The Art of Abingdon

JOHN McLELLAN

MOTOR RACING PUBLICATIONS LTD
28 Devonshire Road, Chiswick, London W4 2HD, England

ISBN 0 900549 45 9
First published 1982

Photosetting by Zee Creative Ltd, London SW16
Monochrome origination by The Purchasing Link Ltd., Warlingham, Surrey ·
Printed in Great Britain by Page Bros. (Norwich) Ltd., Norwich, Norfolk

Contents

This book is dedicated to all who contributed to the design, production, tuning and maintenance of MGs with such skill and dedication for more than half a century on behalf of enthusiastic owners and admirers throughout the world.

Introduction

At the end of August 1979 the small English country town of Abingdon prepared to celebrate the 50th Anniversary, the Golden Jubilee, of the sports-car factory that had provided a good living and a fair measure of prosperity for the local populace. In the long years since the first MGs were built, the Morris Garages marque had had its ups and downs. There had been periods of uncertainty, especially in the mid-1970s, when it seemed that the honoured name would disappear. By 1978 there was a new feeling of optimism, born of a new policy introduced by BL Limited's chief executive, Sir Michael Edwardes. Individual makes were to be promoted strongly once again, the shapeless Leyland Cars grouping was to disappear. Symbols like MG's octagon were to take on a new importance.

Within hours, it seemed, the enthusiastic MG people had put this policy into action. Octagons sprouted on the Abingdon factory buildings, a huge sign announced that here was the home of MG sports cars.

And so MG workers and the townsfolk set to work to make the first week of September 1979 a memorable celebration. If there was any euphoria, it was to be short-lived. The following week it was announced that Abingdon was to be closed. BL Cars, fighting a rearguard battle to protect its falling market share, had come to believe that in an industry where production rates of less than around a quarter-of-a-million a year were considered to be uneconomic, the less than a thousand-cars-a-week MG factory was an anachronism.

The flood of protest and noisy derision which this decision caused was remarkable and led to a determined but ultimately unsuccessful rescue attempt by the management of Aston Martin Lagonda. This powerful response came as no surprise to those who have observed the enormous enthusiasm that exists worldwide for MG sports cars. Within the Abingdon factory itself there was also a strong feeling of personal commitment, even extending to the string of managers who were sent by the parent corporation to serve their time there after the retirement of the greatly respected John Thornley. More than that, the vast number of enthusiasts who have owned, driven or admired MG sports models all around the world represented an enormous reservoir of goodwill for the make.

It was an interest that extended not only to the cars, but to the small Thames-side town they came from and even to the country roads that surround it. The strong sense of identification with the make felt by so many people who have worked at Abingdon also meant that a valuable archive was collected together. Engineers and designers have always been prepared to discuss recent or distant MG history. Much statistical information has thus been preserved and in the photographic department over at the Cowley plant owned by the parent BL Cars are negatives in their thousands covering most aspects of the MG story.

Naturally there have been very many books about MG, ranging from Barre Lyndon's famous sponsored sequence of volumes recounting the exploits of Kimber's heyday in the mid-1930s which included that tantalizing speculation at the end of *Circuit Dust* that suggested that the company might just have had a Grand Prix contender in mind in 1934. John Thornley's fascinating *Maintaining The Breed* told the story of MG racing cars from the tentative beginnings in the 1920s through to the 1950s and in his detailed appendices he provided the skeleton of technical fact which subsequent authors have clothed to taste.

Kenneth Ullyett's *The MG Companion* of 1960 was a factual study of the MG up to the MGA. The definitive history appeared with Wilson McComb's *The Story of The MG Sports Car,* since reissued and expanded under the title *MG by McComb.* There have been literally thousands of articles and shorter studies over the years and this author gladly acknowledges his debt to the informative journals produced by the many branches of the MG Car Club. In recent years the reduction in cost of lithographic printing has enabled large, well-illustrated works such as Richard Knudson's and Michael Allison's to become available at accessible prices. But for all of us who write about motor cars and for whom life is just too short to sample all of them, try as we might, the greatest thanks must go to the journalists who spent so many hours tapping out their impressions and views of the MG cars they examined in the factory or at motor shows, watched in competitions, or drove on test for their journals.

My thanks also go to those enthusiastic engineers and designers at Abingdon, Cowley and Longbridge, who were prepared to take the time to discuss topics that needed illumination during my time at British Leyland and BL Ltd. I also had the great good fortune to be able to tape-record interviews with some of the respected figures who achieved so much with such limited resources at MG. Special thanks are due to John Cooper and his helpful staff in the photographic services unit at Cowley and to the photographers whose professional skills and judgment make the Cowley archives so valuable.

I was fortunate enough to be involved in the creation of Leyland Historic Vehicles under the leadership of Alex Park and am deeply grateful for the helpfulness of the staff of that company and its successor, BL Heritage Ltd, who now administer so much priceless material, and in particular my thanks goes to Anders Clausager, the company's archivist, for permission to browse and study so many original documents.

Peter Jewson (J2), David Wood (Midget) and Sue Saxton (MGB) earn my gratitude for providing the cars which are featured on the jacket of this book in the photograph taken so artistically by Graham Murrell, to whom I am also most grateful, while I am indebted to my publisher, John Blunsden, for the benefit of his editorial guidance and the provision of material from his personal archive.

Finally, I am most thankful of all that whilst MGs, sadly, are no longer made at Abingdon, at least that famous octagonal badge has been reborn in a car which would seem to have a genuine MG character. If the MG Metro 1300, and the other MG models which are planned to follow it, can reveal evidence of the special extra ingredient provided for half a century by that unique Art of Abingdon, they will be fine cars indeed.

JOHN McLELLAN

Abingdon, 1982

MG — The Art of Abingdon

CHAPTER ONE

Bullnose and flatnose

When William Richard Morris began to make Morris cars in Oxford in 1913 he built well. He had observed for himself that the new mass-production manufacturers in the USA — Ford, the Dodge brothers, Hupp — constructed cars that were as robust and trouble-free as their designers could contrive. Their enormous success did not come from cutting corners off the quality, but from efficient manufacture of a simple, practical product in enormous quantities. With that single object in view Morris went into production with his own light car and was to become a major force in the British and European motor industry by the mid-1920s. Since his cars were both soundly designed and properly made of good materials it was natural that enthusiastic owners should think of using them in a sporting way.

In 1914 Cowley offered a neat single-seater Sporting model on the Oxford De Luxe chassis. Fitted with a side-valve White and Poppe four-cylinder 60 × 90 mm, 1,018-cc engine and a rear axle of 3.5:1 ratio, the whole outfit 'specially picked and tuned-up', the Sporting cost £220 fully equipped. It was not particularly successful, for only a few were sold, but it may well be considered to be the first ancestor of the MG. More than that, Morris had demonstrated his understanding of the useful marketing fact that it was possible to ask a premium price for a higher-performance derivative of the bread-and-butter line. The Sporting, with much less elaborate body than the ordinary De Luxe two-seater tourer and less fully equipped, cost some £20 more than its sister.

There were to be other similar sporting Morris variants. A Sports Cowley was sold between 1921 and 1923 with a mildly tuned engine and a higher back-axle ratio than standard. It, too, sold at a premium £398 10s (£398.50) to the £375 of the standard two-seater. There was an Oxford Sports model in 1923, and several examples of these competed in trials and speed events in the 1920s. Possibly the most highly developed of the Oxfords was that of Wellsteed, which lapped Brooklands in

the hands of Paul in 1928 at a thoroughly respectable 78.31 mph.

Since it is evident that Morris, whatever his reservations about motor racing may have been, was sympathetic to the idea that some of his products could be sold with a sporting image, it merely needed the right man to find his way into the organization for something interesting to start. That man was Cecil Kimber, born of a family of modestly middle-class origins; an enthusiastic motorcyclist in his teens, he carried a steel plate in his thigh and a limp to mark his enthusiasm. At the end of the 1914-18 war he was 25 years old, with a solid engineering background in the Sheffield Simplex and E. C. Wrigley concerns. Wrigley supplied engines and gearboxes to William Morris, the two men met and Kimber impressed Morris sufficiently to be offered a position within the fast-expanding Morris empire at Oxford, which by now included not only the car plant down at the end of the Cowley road, but a whole network of workshops, showrooms and garages in the centre of the old university city.

Kimber went to the Morris Garages concern as sales manager and in 1922, on the unexpected death of his superior, he took over as general manager. Not content merely to tend the conglomeration of machinery which Town and Gown sent into the clutter of workshops at the back of the Clarendon Hotel in Oxford, he started to experiment. He had a liking for designing sporty bodies and it was one of these, a yellow two-seater with a long tail, sloping windscreen with triangular side panels, and scuttle ventilators, which took the fancy of undergraduate Oliver Thirkell when he saw it in the Cornmarket showroom priced at £300, in the summer of 1923. He can be called the first MG customer, for this Morris Cowley Special from Morris Garages was really the start of the true MG story.

The great years of the MG coincide exactly with the working careers of two men, and it can surely be no accident that their two characters, though differing in every way except their commitment to hard work and consummate craftsmanship in the pursuit of high performance, seem somehow to be mirrored in the character of the MG cars themselves. To a great degree the story of the MG sports cars from Abingdon is the story of Cec Cousins and Syd Enever.

Cec Cousins always said of himself that he was the first employee of MG and he probably was. A gangling, raw-boned man, in his eighth decade he was still tall enough to dominate any group. He came from Oxford's Walton Street district, a neighbourhood of small homes and resilient working people in an area where wages were never high. He left school at 14 and was apprenticed to T. G. West, general steam and agricultural engineers of the same district. In 1920 he went off to Morris Garages at Clarendon Yard, working as an improver mechanic — a kind of post-apprentice trainee — on motorcycles. He worked hard, and by the time MG went to its Abingdon factory in 1929 he was foreman of the experimental department, a crucially important job. He completed his long career with the company in 1969 as works manager. His career was paralleled by that of Syd Enever, who was to become one of the designers responsible for the greatest MG achievements and for the development of its longest-lived product, the MGB.

For 51 years, Enever's life was wrapped up in the MG company. Born in Hampshire in 1906, he and his five sisters were brought up by his mother alone. Life was not easy, for they subsisted on a 10s (50p) a week legacy which Mrs Enever supplemented by going out to work while Syd went off to school at three. Later they all moved to Oxford, where Mrs Enever took on a tall house near the theatres and ran it as a theatrical boarding house. Like many a youngster, he built 'go-karts' of wood and pram wheels, even fitting one with wings, 'but it never took off,' he recalled.

In due course he and a friend graduated to building cycles from parts culled from scrap merchants. His school years ended with a second place in class and his headmaster, knowing he was mechanically minded, found him a job in the Morris Garages salesrooms in Queen Street, Oxford at 12s 6d (62½p) a week, under general manager Armstead. After this probationary period he went out to the garages behind the Clarendon Hotel. 'One of the mechanics,' he remembered, 'was a tall fellow called Cecil Cousins.'

Enever started work for foreman 'Copper' Crease, who had begun with William Morris at the Oxford Automobile and Cycle Agency in New Road, Oxford back in 1903. Under his foreman's considerate attention young Enever blossomed, working on a stream of mundane cars ranging from the Belsizes and Singers of the townsmen to the

glamorous Bugattis and Hispano-Suizas of the undergraduates. By this time Armstead had been replaced by the short-lived Anderson, and then by Kimber, who was seen much about the town on a small Triumph motorcycle.

Around 1924, the Clarendon Yard garage was completely reconstructed and covered in, making it a lighter and brighter place to work. The mechanics served weekend duties on rota, and one Sunday, when Enever was standing by, he was confronted by the worried owner of a Morris Cowley which had run a big-end bearing while on a journey with his family. Syd, with the attention to detail that was to be so characteristic, had prepared various items against the day of their possible use. One of these was a big-end bearing. Within some 20 minutes the sump was off, the new bearing fitted and the sump back on. The customer was only too pleased to pay the £4 10s (£4.50) fixed charge for the work and Enever gleefully entered the amount against the 20 minutes the job had taken, much to the consternation of the accounts department, who remembered the feat for years.

In 1926 Enever bought a 3½ hp BSA motorcycle, and soon he was competing in the sidecar events at the local grass-track meetings. It was then that he took his first faltering step to tuning, bolting a steel plate to the piston to raise the compression ratio. 'It worked reasonably well until it melted and ran out of the exhaust pipe,' he commented. He soon found out the correct way to tune engines and learnt the value of torsional stiffness in frames when he built a three-wheeler and had to remove the springs to keep it upright.

An assignment to prepare for sale the stocks of used cars held by Morris Garages led to a visit to the temporarily unused Pavlova factory in Abingdon, for it was here that they were stored. Coming to the conclusion that promotion at the Morris Garages was very much a question of 'dead men's boots', Enever began to look about him. He was offered a job at the Morris factory at Cowley, but instead he took an offer from Kimber, who had heard of him from foreman Crease. When he started at Abingdon early in 1930 George 'Pop' Propert was works manager, and he handed-over Enever to Cousins, now MG experimental department foreman, with the remark, 'Here's a bright boy from the Clarendon, and we want you to look after him'.

Others, too, served long and fruitfully with the company: Reg Jackson and Alec Hounslow were typical of the men whose loyalty and skills made the great successes of the 1930s, 1940s and 1950s possible. They went on to take senior posts in the company.

Meanwhile, Kimber had begun marketing a series of Cowleys with special bodies to his own design built either by the Oxford coachbuilders Raworth or by Carbodies of Coventry, with whom he was to have a fruitful working relationship for the next 12 years. As yet these 'chummy'-bodied versions of the Oxford and Cowley were little more than a profitable sideline for Morris Garages, like the Sporting model of 1914 had been. If, as seems likely, Kimber was able to sell these compact occasional-four-seater cars for close to £300, the revenue was doubly welcome, for by 1923 William Morris was well into the price-cutting campaign that was to bring down the price of the ordinary Cowley from £425 early in 1922 to £195 in 1925.

Certainly, it was one of these Morris Garages Cowley 'chummies' that Kimber drove to a gold medal in the 1923 Land's End Trial. It was lightly tuned for this purpose, but as yet Kimber was paying more attention to looks than performance; he was still offering special bodies rather than special cars. In March 1924 the William Morris-controlled magazine *The Morris Owner* carried an advertisement for a range of MG products and coachwork which included saloons, a landaulette and more lively designs such as a coupe and an open sports model.

In May 1924 the same journal carried an advertisement for a two-seater on a Cowley with special carburettor, flattened road springs and lowered steering wheel to match the special Raworth body. Nearly a year after Thirkell had bought his example, Kimber was still trying to shift the last of that first batch of a half-dozen two-seaters.

'This MG', said the advertising copy, 'Super Sports Morris will climb the famous Porlock Hill at 25 miles per hour. The gradient of this noted acclivity is one in five and the Treasury Rating of the car is only 11.9 hp. It will be seen therefore that the inherent possibilities of the famous Morris engine can be brought out by those who know how.

'Mounted on this out-of-the-ordinary chassis is the most delightful two-seater body imaginable. Beautifully comfortable, with adjustable seat and single dickey, the finish is of the highest class and the style irreproachable. The "Tout Ensemble" is one of the finest productions we have ever turned out from our famous Queen Street showrooms. For a car of such distinction the price, £350, is extraordinarily modest.'

Perhaps it was, but even so the two-seater was not the fastest of sellers. But Kimber was not to be deflected. By the end of June 1924 he had designed and built an open four-seater sports tourer body of truly irresistible distinction. It found its way on to both the four-cylinder chassis and that of Morris' disastrous F-type six-cylinder, the Silent Six, built using a Hotchkiss-designed side-valve engine that had a sad appetite for crankshafts.

To match this excellent coachwork the chassis used by Kimber began to receive more attention, and a tiny workshop in what is now Pusey Lane, Oxford, was taken on. In the 1925 model year the bullnose 14/28 took on its own strong MG identity. There was virtually no mechanical difference from the ordinary Oxford except that rod-operated four-wheel brakes, later with a mechanical servo, were fitted, but some attention to detail in the cylinder-head ensured that the 1,802-cc Oxford engine gave about 35 bhp, rather more than the comfortable but unenterprising 28 bhp of the standard version. To match, there were the by now customary flatter road springs, and better shock absorbers were fitted.

As well as a four-seater tourer a neat two-seater was offered, and closed models included the odd-looking Salonette, which was a two-door saloon with a tiny pointed tail. Prices ranged from £375 for the tourer to £475 for the Salonette when it first appeared.

CHAPTER TWO

Majestic sixes — Minor fours

The 14/28 cars were exceedingly handsome, especially when they used the long 108-in-wheelbase Oxford chassis available during the 1925 and 1926 seasons. But still they were only pleasingly modified versions of a standard mass-production car. If Kimber's reputation were to depend solely on these cars it is quite likely that the MG name would have remained in the records simply as an obscure firm of specialist coachbuilders operating from a mews in Oxford, a forgotten off-shoot of the early empire of William Morris. The same is true of Sir William Lyons, whose Swallow bodies hardly made him a true manufacturer until the advent of the SS1 in 1933. In a more modern context, specialist tuners such as Sprinzel or Ralph Broad's Broadspeed outfit were to do much more to the cars they prepared for racing and rallying than ever Kimber and his team essayed in the early days, yet nobody claims either of these determined gentlemen were motor manufacturers. It needed something more, and that something was already being produced slowly, first at the old livery stable turned garage in Longwall Street, where many of the early 'chummies' were made, and later at Pusey Street.

Kimber's Special FC 7900 was in its essentials a Morris, but those essentials were used in a new way, a way that was to be more characteristic of the 1930s production at Abingdon than it was of the operations in Oxford. It used a four-cylinder, chain-driven overhead-valve engine of 11.9 hp built by the Hotchkiss company and first seen at Olympia in 1920. It was originally used for the Scottish-built Gilchrist car, of which some 200 examples were built. The engine was installed in a chassis consisting of the front half of a Cowley united to a specially built rear-end permitting regular half-elliptic springs to be used all round. Morris Oxford brakes and a steel-panelled grand-sport-type two-seater body completed the outfit.

To bring the car into the 1,500-cc class for trials the engine had been sleeved to bring it back to the earlier Cowley's displacement of 69 × 100 mm, or 1,496 cc. There was a three-speed gearbox, and since the engine was capable of 3,500 rpm a top speed of some 70 mph was possible. In the Land's End Trial, which he reached after the almost-mandatory last-minute rush when a chassis-member had cracked, Kimber made no mistakes. Reporting on the event, *The Motor* said of Beggar's Roost: 'This formidable test hill reared skywards from Barbrook Mill and those waiting their turn to ascend could almost see the floorboards of the cars climbing the red and rocky precipice. The hill was roped off and clear of spectators, who thronged the banks in thousands and although the surface was loose and in places very soft, owing to its having been churned up by the rear wheels of sidecar outfits . . . Kimber (MG sports) made a fairly good ascent although he looked somewhat worried.'

Kimber seems promptly to have lost interest in his little Special, for he sold it soon after the trial; much more elaborate machines were on his mind. Towards the end of the following year Morris dropped the bullnose bonnet shape and for the 1927 season introduced a stiffer and heavier chassis frame with half-elliptic arrangement that had previously been something of a handicap to MG's efforts to improve rear-end stability. Five-stud wheels and a rubber-mounted steering box

appeared, the latter soon being amended by MG and becoming a solidly mounted Marles unit.

The moves to improve steering and roadholding were shrewd, for the new car was 2½ cwt heavier in the chassis, and its bodywork was also heavier, since it was bigger. Although now dubbed 14/40 and despite a new exhaust manifold, the engine was little more powerful than before at around 35 bhp, so it was in areas other than sheer performance that the flatnose MG model had to excel. The new body was finished in a remarkably handsome display of engine-turned polished aluminium side panels combined with rich red or blue steel upper panels. Perhaps it was just a little less appealing than the 1924-25 tourer, but the MGs' popularity and sales were maintained. Sir William Morris allowed Kimber to build a new factory at Edmund Road, Cowley, at a cost of £16,000 out of the MG profits, and for two years from September 1927 all the 14/40 production was from there. With the whole operation under one roof, and with adequate space for the first time, production benefited, with some 400 cars rolling out during 1928.

Possibly Kimber was misled by the success of his well-set-up fast tourers, a success aided by the steady downwards drift of their prices — the tourer was down to £360 in 1925 and £350 two years later — for he began to think of moving into the quality sports-car market. In retrospect it was one of the most risky decisions any car maker could have taken at that time for although the slump had not yet begun the market was by no means buoyant in 1928. Certainly Kimber must have had some kind of approval from Sir William Morris for what by MGs standards was likely to be a lengthy and costly programme.

Morris himself hung on too long to his medium-priced cars and at the end of the 1920s he began to see his share of the market slip badly. By 1928 the Morris salesmen were also uneasy about their exposed position in the 11-to-13-hp popular-car bracket. Their nearest rivals were Austin, and they were doing quite well with the little Seven, the leader in the so-called baby-car class with its miniature side-valve 750-cc engine, whilst the Longbridge flanks were protected by a range of larger vehicles such as the 12/4, a popular competitor to the Cowley. A large six-cylinder engine seemed one solution, permitting as it would the addition of up-market luxury cars, to sell under the Morris name at a slight premium, as well as powering any other entirely different model that might seem desirable. Such a model was the one on Kimber's mind, and when Morris Engines Branch in Coventry delivered the new six-cylinder engine it proved to be a fine chain-driven overhead-camshaft unit with very slightly inclined valves and a bottom-end conducive to thoughts of high speeds.

Inevitably, with an engine of such origins, there were compromises. It was intended to be paired with a three-speed gearbox in the Morris application; it was fashionable to claim of 'sixes' that they were so flexible in performance that it was never necessary to change gear. It was desirable to keep the annual tax low and that depended on a formula which took into account bore but not stroke, and the end-product was an engine with the longest stroke ever installed in any MG; it was 110 mm, and with a bore of 69 mm the swept volume was 2,468 cc.

But with its crossflow cylinder-head and tidy lines it was a fitting powerplant for the substantial MG chassis that was planned for it. Away went the Cowley structure, and in its place was a much more solid construction, one which had some tangible new features. There was a new front axle, and ENV were called in to strengthen the Morris rear axle ready for the extra power transmitted from the new engine.

Kimber was not the man to let such a fine new chassis be undermined by any failure to ensure that the car's looks were in keeping. When the new Mark I appeared in late-summer of 1928 it was provided with the first example of the distinctive radiator-shell treatment that was to become synonymous with MG. It was his own personal touch on what was by now very much a corporate Morris and MG production, calling on facilities that were open to him at various factories in the rambling parent organization. The corporate approach had one disadvantage in that the gearbox was of necessity the standard product with its long, cranked gear-lever and — for a sporting car — unsuitably wide ratios. And there were only three speeds.

Titled the MG 18/80 Six and shown at the London Motor Show at Olympia that autumn, the new model was supported by a superbly finished show chassis and was accepted as being designed and built to the highest standards. Fast and accelerative by previous MG yardsticks, it clung to the road with remarkable fervour. The Carbodies-built open tourers were admirably proportioned, instrumentation and equipment was of the best, and altogether the 18/80 came in for much favourable comment. It was expensive at £485, and was set to become more so, but it was in an interesting segment of the market and had little

competition. The twin-camshaft Sunbeam 3-litre was costly and handicapped by an antiquated chassis, Bentley was moving up-market away from the 3-litre, and there were continentals ranging from the Delage 14/40 of 2.2 litres — which was shortly to be dropped — to the Bugatti T43 of 2.3 litres. None of these could be said to be aimed at the same potential buyer as the MG.

It was indeed the keen price of £555 which aroused the immediate approval of *The Motor* when they road-tested a four-door saloon in March 1928: '. . . the bodywork was of an extremely high order'. The gearbox called for little comment, except to say: 'The control is centrally placed and cranked well back so that there is no necessity for the driver to lean forward when effecting gear changes.' They thought that despite its sporting pretensions the 18/80 behaved like a touring car. 'There is no need for one constantly to change gear, for the speed range is from 5 mph to 78 mph in top gear.'

The suspension, too, was well-liked. Describing the shackles of the half-elliptics as being at the front of the springs, 'to minimize the effects of spring deflection on braking and steering', they thought that although the ride was best above 30 mph, it was an excellent all-round compromise.

The road-testers were often content not to wander too far from home in those days, and when it came to describing the Mark I's hill-climbing capabilities they were satisfied to cite the performance on Stokenchurch Hill on the main road between Oxford and London, which, 'despite the fact that it has some acute bends, did not fetch the car down below 40 mph, on top gear — a very good performance'.

Despite such accolades the car was not so successful as the earlier 14/28-cum-14/40 series had been. They had sold close to a thousand in three years, but it took nearly five years to sell less than 800 of the two 18/80 variants. The MG team had been caught up in the classic dilemma of the late-1920s car designer; they believed that customers wanted ever greater performance and standards of equipment, and they had to provide more complex, more powerful engines to maintain the speed and acceleration that seemed necessary. Higher performance with bigger structures led to hefty brakes and much stouter road springs to control the loads they imposed. Chassis-frames had to be made much stronger to maintain all this careful engineering in some kind of accurate relationship with itself. Many designers did not break free of this spiral, and indeed in 1929 and again in 1930 Kimber was to carry on designing in this philosophy.

Had the 18/80 and the 14/40 models been the only exhibits on the MG stand at the London Motor Show in 1928 there can be little doubt that the marque MG would now be little more than a fond memory, respected only for a handful of surviving side-valve tourers and Salonettes and a smaller number of beautifully executed 'sixes'.

But there were also the little M-type Midgets. In appearance small-scale replicas of the 'sixes', but with tiny two-seater bodies, they were powered by an overhead-camshaft engine of 850 cc; it was a startling change of direction which took the MG management out of the potentially fatal spiral into which it had slipped and opened up a market of gigantic potential. The decision to build the Midget ensured the survival of Kimber's five-years-old marque and was to lead to a remarkable series of sports-racing designs. Its arrival was well-judged, for there was already a thriving small sports-car market in Britain. At 1,100-cc level it had been served by imported French Salmsons and Amilcars, simple in concept and sometimes crude in execution, but very pretty in a light-aircraft kind of way with their pointed-tail two-seater bodies and steeply raked vee windscreens. In the smaller 750-cc category the Austin Seven in a myriad of disguises served pretty well. To own a Gordon England Cup Sports or Austin's own Super Sports model was the ambition of thousands of comparatively less-well-off young drivers.

The Midget slotted into this market very nicely. At £185 it was cheaper than both the imports — usually around £250 — and Austin's sporting offerings at £225. Although with its compact 78-in wheelbase it could hardly match the easy gait of the longer-wheelbase French cars, the Midget was a practical and comfortable little car for two people who had no objection to close quarters. Press and public alike were highly favourable, and when the new Midget began to show well in events such as the Land's End Trial and the JCC's High-Speed Trial at Brooklands, success seemed certain.

In November 1928, two months after the Midget's announcement, the company ran an audacious advertisement in *The Morris Owner:* 'Erected entirely in the MG Model Works — unique in being the only factory in the world entirely devoted to the production of Sports Cars — this latest addition to the MG range is destined to make motoring history. It is not a ''hotted up'' touring chassis, but is produced exclusively and specifically to provide a high sporting

performance.' Arguably that copy could have been applied to the 18/80, but never to the M-Type Midget. Certainly the car would make motoring history, but if ever a car was essentially a special-bodied touring chassis it was that first Midget. They may have flattened the road springs a little to lower it, and the steering column was certainly raked, but the rest was purest Morris Minor.

The relationship of the Midget to the Minor was the same as that of the 1924 MG Super Sports to the original Oxford, but in the Midget's case the additional sales at a premium price must have been very welcome to the Minor's builders at Cowley, for the Minor was never able to crack the Austin Seven's hold on the baby-car market. Although it offered a slightly bigger engine with overhead valves and a footbrake on all four wheels plus slightly better roadholding against the Austin's side valves and more primitive brakes, the Minor was not a great success. Even the 1930 adventure of the £100 Minor — a loss-leader if ever there was one — did not help. But in four years the Midget sold 3,200-odd, and profitability must have been very comfortable.

Meanwhile, Kimber took another step in the six-cylinder spiral with the magnificent 18/80 Mark II. There was a yet stiffer frame, axles that left behind their origins with a track four inches wider than that of the Oxford and the old 18/80 and, most important of all, a four-speed gearbox with a carefully engineered remote-control gear-lever. In *The Motor's* June 1930 road-test of a two-seater tourer there is a consistently enthusiastic atmosphere. They had driven the car for the unusually long distance of 2,000 miles, and that had included competing in the Land's End Trial during the Easter weekend. They were much taken with its third gear, finding that 60 mph was possible in this high indirect speed.

In contrast with the Mark I, the Mark II gearbox positively welcomed use: '. . . one changes speed for the sheer fun of it, snicking into ''second'' quite unnecessarily to round street corners and dropping into ''third'' every time one wishes to overtake another vehicle'.

By the time this report appeared Kimber had advanced yet further with the 18/100 Mark III, designed as an out-and-out road-racing car. The engine was tuned and converted to dry-sump lubrication and the objective was to obtain a car that in broad terms had 100 hp and 100 mph available. In fact the development period was protracted, and it is evident that lubrication problems proved intractable. The Shell company assisted in this programme, which, given the calibre of the engineers, would have been successful in time. Cousins recalled many years later the long hours spent while they were trying to find that elusive high-speed reliability after the 1930 Double Twelve at Brooklands. A typical sequence involved leaving Abingdon for Engines Branch at Coventry and returning via Abingdon for a 12-hour high-speed run on the Outer Circuit at Brooklands, followed by an immediate return to Coventry for an all-night engine examination and test. There was an early start the next morning, with a call for breakfast at home *en route* to Brooklands for another 12-hour test drive. Not surprisingly the 18/100 was an expensive car — nearly 30 years were to pass before, with the introduction of the Twin Cam in 1958, MG prices rose again to anything like the same level.

Meanwhile, to help brighten the sales prospects for some of the Mark I chassis still encumbering Abingdon, a slender four-seater sports-tourer body was designed and built by Carbodies. The Speed Model was announced in September 1930, ready for the 1931 selling season. It weighed 22¾ cwt without occupants and this lively combination of a smooth six-cylinder engine and a light body produced one of the most satisfying of all the many variations on the 18/80 theme. In its road-test of the £525 Speed Model, *The Motor* commented that the Dewandre vacuum-servo mechanism was one of the most notable of all improvements to the chassis. 'The easy brake operation makes the car quite effortless to drive compared with the earlier models on which a certain amount of energy had to be expended on braking.'

The Speed Model was offered with a guaranteed 80 mph top speed, and the road-test car exceeded this figure over the measured half-mile, no doubt aided by the reduced wind-resistance of the narrow body, with its outside handbrake and cut-out for the driver's elbow.

The provision of racing-type Rudge Whitworth wire wheels also rated mention: '. . . fitted as standard — a luxury not usually encountered on cars of this price'.

Meanwhile, the success of the Midget and a growing amount of service activity had made a yet larger factory necessary, and in September 1929 MG production had been transferred to what was to become its permanent base at Abingdon. At the end of Cemetery Road, Abingdon, the Pavlova Leather Company had some big factory buildings which had lain empty since the demand for leather Army overcoats had dwindled with the signing of

the Armistice in 1918, and it was in these well-constructed buildings that MG found a home.

CHAPTER THREE

The works goes racing

The M-type Midget blossomed very quickly, becoming accepted as a true sports car almost immediately. The need for stunt demonstrations such as the 100 ascents of the Beggars Roost trials hill in the summer of 1930 soon receded as the little car began to fulfil its promise. *The Morris Owner* had announced the introduction of the car as the Morris Midget, but the sporting world soon welcomed it as an MG. Five were entered in each of the MCC's and the JCC's High-Speed Trials at Brooklands in 1929 and picked up 10 gold medals, putting up first, second and third fastest times in the latter while they were about it. At the heart of the matter was the willing little powerplant, which accepted tuning with almost ludicrous ease compared with the thoroughly costly process that developing the six-cylinder engine had proved to be.

The Midget weighed 10 cwt 20 lb when *The Motor* road-tested it in July 1929, not long after it was introduced. 'The real charm of this amazing little car, however, is on the open road, and driven properly it takes a particularly fast car to pass it. It has a maximum speed of 65 mph, although the makers conservatively claim only 60 mph, and can be driven at this pace with every feeling of safety', they commented, and it was all achieved on the modest 20 bhp that the conservative valve timing permitted.

With modified timing, which boosted output to 27 bhp, the Midgets took the team prize in the JCC Double Twelve race, and they were then called 12/12 Midgets when produced in replica form. One of these machines covered 22 laps of Brooklands at a 62.87-mph average (a standard M-type did a lap at 53.55 mph) and they began to appear in every type of competition in the hands of enthusiastic owners, at which point they revealed their limitations; the mildly improved Minor chassis was really not entirely happy at speeds of 70 mph and above, and clearly something new was needed if Abingdon was to reap the benefits due to it from Kimber's inspired decision to make the M-type.

It was a difficult moment for the company.

Poised to enter the 1930s and facing a deep trade recession the effects of which they had so far managed to fend-off, thanks to the backing of Sir William Morris and the brisk sales of the Midget, they had a range that was seriously compromised in one direction or another.

The 14/40, the Mark I and the Midget were all betrayed by their touring-car mechanicals, while the Mark II and the 18/100 were superlative cars, but ruinously expensive to make and to buy. Some way had to be found to combine the low price and brisk sales of the Midget with the technical excellent of the flagships of the range.

Since the small French models had dominated the 1,100-cc sports class through the 1920s, it was to them that Kimber and his team turned, for they were fast and highly controllable little cars. With the exception of miniature Grand Prix types, such as the Amilcar G6, they were also very cheap. Abingdon took a look at a 1,500-cc Alfa-Romeo and then by good luck or judgment happened on a late-series Rally, which was produced as a typical pointed-tail Grand Sport two-seater looking just like a miniature Bugatti. Into the factory this went, to be most carefully examined. The whole point of the little Rally chassis was that it was exceedingly low. Just aft of the front springs it dog-legged down and then ran back practically straight below the rear axle. All the road springs were outrigged, short and virtually flat. The engine, a short four-cylinder overhead-valve unit, was low-slung, well back in the frame, and its minimal sump called for an oil tank cradled between the dumbirons ahead of the radiator.

There was no remote-control for the gearbox, but the whole outfit, with its brake rods carried outside the chassis members and its stiff square-tube cross-members, bore the stamp of racing experience.

To their everlasting credit, the MG mechanics adopted most of the features of the chassis, only improving it where they could see the need. Manufacturing simplicity dictated that the chassis be given round tubes for the cross-members, and no doubt with memories of the rear-end steering experienced on the old MG chassis — Midget and Six alike — conventional spring shackles were dispensed with in favour of the sliding trunnions at the rear of the road springs that were destined to make such a contribution to the roadholding of the new Midget family. Such a chassis was stiff neither in beam nor in torsion, but that mattered very little since it was the intention of Hubert Charles, the designer, to fit only the simplest of bodies to the chassis in the beginning, and with the use of a very long bonnet, to reduce the proportion of the wheelbase along which more elaborate bodies would be attached.

The first of these chassis was used for a car that was given the identification EX 120. With the ordinary radiator and a pointed-tail body it was used to cover considerable test mileage in the latter part of 1930. It represented an interesting new development in that the engine and gearbox were securely attached to each other to provide a long stiff beam structure to which the radiator was secured directly at the front. It was a concept that had been used most successfully by Talbot designer Roesch. With the movement of the axles controlled well enough by the design of the spring trunnions it was unnecessary to provide a rigid and therefore heavy chassis structure. The conception was good enough to serve MG until their engines became so powerful five years later that a completely new approach was desirable.

By December 1930 a highly tuned version of the M-type engine was ready to be installed in the car for an attempt on 750-cc class records, for which purpose it was equipped with a special crankshaft and linered down to 81 × 54 mm bore and stroke. Records held by the Austin 750-cc cars were broken at speeds up to 87.11 mph. There was now much speculation as to which marque would be the first to break records at over 100 mph with a 750-cc car — the publicity value would be enormous — and a supercharged version of the engine was prepared. Once again careful experimentation on oils and fuel mixes was undertaken, and companies such as Shell and Castrol were deeply involved. In February 1931 Eyston drove the car at Montlhéry to become the first man to set records at over 100 mph in the class.

Delighted with this result, Kimber organized a grand luncheon at Abingdon in March 1931 and invited the racing world to come along to see EX 120 and a sample chassis of the new C-type Montlhéry Midget. This chassis was equipped with a blown engine, but the first C-types were produced with the unblown units. The price was to be £295 in ready-to-race trim and the response was so strong that a collection of 14 of them was rushed through to completion within two weeks, to be ready for the 1931 Double Twelve race. In Thornley's words, 'split-pinned and wired in every hole', and with every thought given to fitness for the job, the cars were powered by a 750-cc engine that reverted to 57 × 73 mm bore and stroke, there was a tough ENV four-speed box with remote gearlever, and a reserve oil-tank fed through a float chamber to keep oil at the correct level in the sump. There were duplicated fuel and ignition circuits — Brooklands was merciless in revealing weaknesses.

In the event the Midgets dominated the field, the Earl of March and C. S. Staniland winning outright at 65.62 mph and the cars taking the team award. It was the beginning of a remarkable period in motor racing history for the MG works, and a horde of private owners went out to race and win at every possible venue. In some respects that horde of owners tended to overshadow the very real achievement of the MGs at the time, for there was a tendency to think that with so many of them competing it was almost inevitable that they should win regularly.

The company traded on the success of the racers, building an enormous variety of production cars bearing a close affinity to the competition versions. Initially, and clearly with the lesson of the M-type well and truly learnt, the smaller cars were built down to a price and the first of the new 1,271-cc six-cylinder models introduced in late-1931 had bodies of the utmost simplicity of construction. With engines derived from the M-type and a chassis essentially a 'stretched' C-type, the F-type Magna was supported by a four-cylinder D-type Midget and sold briskly enough for a year at between £215 and £289, depending on whether open or closed, or two or four-seater bodywork was specified.

By the time the C-type Midget was road-tested by *The Autocar* in November 1931 the price was up to £575 in blown form, which is hardly surprising in view of the considerable amount of preparation and the high finish imparted to the car. Its best speed over the Brooklands half-mile was 87.8 mph, running on a 80/20 per cent petrol/benzole mix. It is clear that the engine was on the inflexible side. 'One would not expect the slow running in top or even third gear to be good; but in fact no-one interested in a car of this nature would want to make it run slowly on the higher ratios.' The weight was 13 cwt and the normal limit for the engine was quoted as 5,500 rpm. The testers thought it a very 'British' kind of car.

In blown form the C-type was thirsty, and large slab-tanks mounted transversely behind the seats became the wear for long-distance races after the 1932 Ulster TT. They helped to simplify the bodywork, too.

When the next development of the Midget appeared in autumn 1932 it had just such a body

and an unblown engine giving a lusty 36 bhp by grace of much more robust internals. Its wheelbase was 86 in, and its track 42 in. There was now a crossflow cylinder-head and a more sporting camshaft profile. With its long, lean bonnet and skinny 4.50 x 19 tyres the J2 Midget, very much the brainchild of Charles and Enever, became, at £199.10s (£199.50) the archetypal MG for two generations of young enthusiasts.

By 1932 the C-derived Magic Midget, EX 127, had been developed into the world's fastest 750-cc car. It was built in 1931 and with it the MG works began to move towards a more scientific school of design for their racing cars. Certainly the chassis-frame, essentially still that of the C-type, had no such pretension, but the long, high-tailed body was about as aerodynamically clean as any exposed-wheel car could ever hope to be, and the transmission was schemed to allow the driver to sit centrally, low behind the engine; the cross-sectional area was pretty well reduced to that of the driver himself.

There was scientific thought in abundance in the highly stressed 750-cc engine. Magic Midget in the hands of Eyston and Denly took flying-mile and kilometre records at over 120 mph, and shortly afterwards took the 12-hours record at close to 90 mph despite many stops to replenish with oil when the sorely stressed rear-main-bearing housing broke-up. During the same raid on Montlhéry a stripped J3 Midget took the 24-hours record and gave to MG every record in its class.

From the J3 was derived the fire-eating J4, which appeared in 1932. This was the ultimate version of the two-bearing Morris Minor engine, and rejoiced in such additional details as thicker cylinder-head studs to withstand the pressures generated by the Powerplus supercharger blowing at up to 18 psi as well as a fully counterbalanced crankshaft machined from a solid billet to ensure rigidity and reduce the loadings on the rear main. Initially it gave 72 bhp at 6,000 rpm, but more was to come if owners accepted a sharply attenuated life for the engine. The J4 was probably one good example of the perils that lie in wait for designers who allow engine power to outrun chassis capabilities, for only a very few brave souls were able to drive it as it demanded.

Quite apart from the Midgets, there was an array of larger six-cylinder-engined designs. Derived from the F-type Magna and the D-type Midget, they were a bewildering assortment of aggressively styled vehicles which, despite carrying, for the greater part, over-weight bodies, still managed to create a certain aura. Their chassis-frames were essentially larger-scale versions of the C-type Midget's and their engines, although originally owing much to the Wolseley 'six' which had powered the derided Hornet, were rapidly changed into free-revving units more to the liking of the Abingdon perfectionists.

In its standard form the F-type's engine gave little more power than that of the J2, but with its well-judged gearbox ratios it performed so pleasingly that its limited roadholding and eight-inch brakes could perhaps be overlooked. The L-type Magna of 1933 was also equipped with an unimpressive chassis (although with 12-inch brakes) but had the robust 1,087-cc Wolseley-built K-series engine. It was given some highly presentable bodies. Both ranges sold briskly, the F-type doing better with 1,250 sold during its year, the L-type nearly 580 in the same period, despite their stock Wolseley Hornet axles giving a track of just 42 inches.

In its September 1933 road-test of the L2 Magna, *The Autocar* had this to say of the 1,087-cc two-seater with its J2 body: 'This modern six-cylinder engine in the Magna is a fine design and it runs with notable smoothness right throughout its range, from a comfortable toddle on top gear right up to nearly 6,000 rpm when all-out'. All-out in this case was 77.50 mph over the measured half-mile with the screen down.

The British were very prone to this kind of small, low-geared sports car. The Triumph Southern Cross was of 1,018 cc, the later Monte Carlo of 1,087 cc and costing £325. The Riley Nine was also an 1,100-cc model, and available with sports tourer bodies by March or in Lynx form before the Imp appeared at around £300. The Singer Nine, available in open and closed 972-cc form, was the car the Midget had to beat, while the 1½-litre six-cylinder Le Mans was still opposition for the Magnas and Magnettes with an 84 mph top speed and a £375 price tag.

The great success of the 750-cc cars in racing and record-breaking — Midgets had won the team prize in the 1930 Double Twelve race, the first five places in general classification in that race the next season, the Irish Grand Prix and the Tourist Trophy outright, third place and the team award in the 500-Miles at Brooklands, all in 1931, and had taken third in the Brooklands 1,000-miles, third in the Tourist Trophy, first, the team award and first three places in class in the 500-miles race in 1932 — meant that the handicappers were certain to tighten the screw.

The new toy was the K-series 1,087-cc Magnette, a last-minute show surprise in October 1932. A conventional MG chassis was improved with bigger brakes and a steering layout designed to correct the basic problem presented by the otherwise neat transverse-drag-link arrangement, namely that the end attached to the nearside stub-axle was expected to move up and down, while that coupled to the steering-column drop-arm had to swing through an arc. Clearly *The Motor's* reporter did not understand the new feature, merely observing: 'A divided track-rod for which many advantages are claimed', was fitted. But in fact the use of a control-arm mounted about one-third of the way along the axle-beam to which the two inboard ends of the divided track-rod were attached, certainly did all that had been hoped for. The brakes, too, were big and electron light-alloy drums helped to keep down unsprung weight.

It was evident that the engine would have a racing future. 'The overhead-camshaft engine of this series is entirely new, consequently there is a very big margin of safety as produced in unsupercharged form. In other words, it is not a "hotted-up" touring car power unit but a racing engine adapted for everyday sporting and touring purposes.' This was indeed a powerful unit in its later forms, with a crossflow head and porting arranged to be able to cope with the abundant gas-flow of a supercharger. The porting led to certain problems, for idling speeds were on the high side, and since the intention was to make the Wilson preselector gearbox available, valve timing had to be mild to give smooth low-speed running.

Long and low, the K-series bodies were right in the fashion set by the SS1 and the four-door pillarless saloon was one of the best-looking cars of its era. MG by now had adopted the bonnet which was carried through to the base of the windscreen on all these models. It improved the appearance of the cars considerably, but despite heavy rubber-sealing arrangements where the bonnet seated on to the bulkhead behind the engine, the saloon tended to be noisy, and fumes found their way into the passenger compartment. There were also a fine range of open sports models, of which the K1 two-seater was a particularly attractive specimen, selling at £360. Regrettably, none of them was a very brisk seller, the back-axle ratio of 4.78:1 perhaps providing an explanation, for although all the cars were capable of 75 mph, the engine was buzzing at high rpm to do it, while *The Light Car* commented on the need to use the gearbox freely.

If the production K-series was not entirely

satisfactory and revealed a need for the supercharger that was so clearly originally intended, there were no reservations at all about the road-racing K3. It was given a Powerplus blower, and its spectacularly successful racing career was to emphasize that power existed in abundance. The model was planned in the late-summer and autumn of 1932 and work accelerated on the project when Earl Howe, who had a pet project to build a British version of the classic Italian road-racing cars such as the eight-cylinder Alfa Romeos, approached Abingdon with the suggestion that he should take a team of cars to the classic Italian Mille Miglia event in the spring of 1933.

The engine was rapidly developed, since it was essentially a six-cylinder, reduced-stroke J4, to cope with the output of the No. 9 Powerplus blower driven via a reduction gear from the front of the crankcase. There was a special forged-steel crankshaft, fully machined and counterbalanced, the main bearings were stiffened and the crankshaft bevel-gears were straight-cut to reduce power losses. There were few suitable gearboxes, for the power was quite possibly going to be as high as 150 bhp, so an ENV-built Wilson preselector box was installed despite its unfavourably wide intermediate ratios.

A first prototype took part in the Monte Carlo Rally in January 1933. The second went out to Italy in late-winter for testing, during which, according to legend, the great Ettore Bugatti took a look at the chassis and condemned the front axle as being too fragile for its task. It is worth recalling that in Barre Lyndon's MG-sponsored book *Circuit Dust,* published soon after the event, this observation is put to the credit of the experienced Tim Birkin, who was one of the team drivers. Apart from the front axle, it was found that second gear was too low, the brake drums were splitting and the steering was being affected by the torque-reaction cables. All these problems were solved before the race, but a persistent problem with spark-plug oiling could not be solved since it was a consequence of the Powerplus eccentric-vane blower's need for oil.

In the race Birkin was sent out to break-up the Maserati opposition, which he did, leaving two cars driven by Eyston/Lurani and Howe/Hamilton to win the 1,100-cc class and the team prize handsomely. It was one of the great achievements of motor racing history — to build, test and modify three cars and take them to a major victory, all between October and May — but yet more was to come.

The K3 was put on offer as a road-racing car at £795, with a typical, neat, slab-tank body, and a total of 31 were built. Owners got 120 bhp at 6,500 rpm, and there was a choice of top gear ratios from 4.3 to 5.7:1. The K3 in its 1933 form was no great prodigy of reliability. Back-axle failure claimed all six entered in the Mannin Beg race, but all else pales beside the achievement in the TT of that year, when the epic struggle on handicap between Nuvolari in Eyston's K3 and Hamilton in the J4 Midget ended with a narrow victory for the former. For 1934, a road-racing body based on that of the Italian Grand Prix cars was evolved, and more development was carried out. A Roots-type Marshall blower was adopted, and although its 10/13 psi pressure gave less power, there was less trouble with plugs. The electron brake drums and steel shoes were replaced by all-steel assemblies and the K3 went on to a long and honourable racing career.

Of all the K3 cars, EX 135, an experimental chassis with offset propeller-shaft built for Eyston, was to have the greatest sequence of successes when it became the Gardner MG in 1938.

In March 1934 a new Midget appeared. With a wheelbase just one-inch longer than that of the J-type, and with the same track for the axles, it weighed 2¼ cwt more than the original cycle-type winged J2 and possessed an engine of the same swept volume, but with three main bearings. The new P-type engine was an altogether more massive construction than the old two-bearing unit, the cylinder-block being designed with an eye to development and offering sufficient rigidity to permit high revolutions. Comparison with the J2 emphasized that the new car was much less spartan, but it was at a disadvantage against opposition such as the 972-cc Singer sports, and in autumn 1935 a bigger-bore 939-cc PB Midget was introduced. First and second gear ratios were higher to produce a very pleasing close-ratio box. It was a very successful small sports car, and in just over two years more than 2,500 of them were sold. Apart from that it provided Enever and his men with a most valuable small racing engine.

In August 1934 a new racing model appeared — the 120 mph-plus 746-cc Q-type, with an engine based on that of the P-type. Like the K3, it was intended for sale, although the £550 asked for it excluded wings and lamps; it was not thought of as a road-going car. The J4 chassis was no longer regarded favourably, and the Zoller-blown Q-type engine went into a K3 chassis to which the lighter N-type axles were fitted. The Zoller could deliver the mixture at up to 28 psi through the gigantic SU carburettor. These were temperamental and demanding engines, and their petrol-alcohol mix was critical.

It was found to be almost impossible to transmit all the power through the preselector gearbox and the rear axle without losing traction or damaging the transmission. An ingenious 'safety valve' clutch was introduced into the transmission to act as a relief if the power fed in exceeded a preset figure. But it was much less easy to prevent the car from twitching itself into a frightening zig-zag motion as it approached its 120 mph maximum on the bumpy Brooklands bankings. Although only raced for a season by the works it showed its potential. Driven by the experienced Everitt, in 1934, it took the 750-cc class standing-start mile record at 85.6 mph. A carefully improved Q-type was built for Harvey-Noble by Robin Jackson, one of the most successful of the Brooklands tuners. Clad in a slender shell reminiscent of a tall 1934 GP Mercedes-Benz, the car took to the track with an engine moved back in the frame and with the K3 front axle installed, both in the interests of stability. It took the Brooklands Outer Circuit class record at over 122 mph. It was evident to Kimber, Charles and Enever that to improve on these performances design had to become as scientific in the chassis as it had become in the engines. The all-independently suspended R-type was put in hand for 1935 and it was intended at first to fit both 1,100-cc and 750-cc engines, according to *The Morris Owner*.

The last of the small six-cylinder cars appeared in April 1934. The chassis was once again more robust and the wheelbase went up to 94 inches with a track of 45 inches. The engine was rubber-mounted at three points and the body was insulated from the racking of the chassis by mounting it on two sub-frames at the side of the chassis, each being attached to the frame by rubber bushes; there was also a flexible mounting at the rear. With the engine now up to 1,271 cc and giving over 56 bhp, performance was much more lively. Since Kimber, with his usual touching faith in the public's desire to buy his cars in saloon form, had once again bought too many of the pillarless saloon bodies, another K generation appeared in mid-1934 with the big K3 brakes. Called the KN, the car was livelier than its predecessors, but the lack of a supercharger still limited its performance. One NA was supercharged by the factory and used in the Monte Carlo Rally by Symons; it gave some 110 bhp at 6,000 rpm and may be regarded as what

would have been possible if the first plans to offer all these K-engined cars in blown form had been carried through.

CHAPTER FOUR
Pushrods and rationalization

1935 is seared into the MG mythology as the year a callously uncaring Lord Nuffield sold out the plucky little MG company to his Morris Organization, delivering it to their profit-obsessed management, there to be dissected, the best parts thrown away and the remainder subjected to rigid control by designers who would be hard put to it to engineer their way out of a paper bag. The notorious decision to abandon MG's intense racing programme is identified as one product of the new regime's hard-heartedness.

But in fact, by 1935, Morris, led by the tough Leonard Lord, had fought their way out of the potentially disastrous position they had found themselves in after the collapse of the popular 11 to 13 hp market in 1930-32. In the new Morris Eight, introduced at the end of 1934, they had a modern small car that was to become a best-seller. Although their range was still too large, it had included some notably successful models. The Isis of 1930, with its JA-series engine from which the 18/80 had earlier been evolved, had a pressed-steel body built with the most up-to-date production techniques and was the first European mass-production car to have hydraulic brakes. Moving production lines had been introduced at Cowley not long after, and the production engineers were progressing steadily towards the chassisless all-steel unitary-construction body. In 1934 the company's sales were up more than 14,000 units to a 58,250 total, and the Ten-Four, with its long-stroke 1,292 cc MPJG engine, sold 12,000 in its first year. Morris said in their publicity: '. . . the greatest manufacturing development in recent years . . . Specialization. One factory produces nothing but engines . . . another concerns itself solely with foundry work . . .'

In contrast, affairs over at Abingdon had a worrying air. Certainly the P-type had been well received by press and public alike. 'Anyone who has had experience of the various preceding Midget models cannot fail to be struck by the very great improvements which this P-type shows in practically all respects over its forerunners,' said *The Autocar* in November 1934.

Using up the remaining closed bodies, the KN was to stay in production, but was hardly in demand despite a facelift, having built a reputation for being fussy to drive, noisy and cramped for four occupants. The N-type, with its rubber-mounted engine and gearbox matched by the flexible body mountings, was a lively car in which most of the shortcomings of the general concept had been corrected. At £305 it was well-finished and equipped. On test with a two-seater in August 1934, *The Autocar* said, '. . . it is a car perfectly suitable for running about, for conveying for instance, an elderly passenger around the country, yet immediately afterwards and without factory experts being in attendance, the car can be put over the half-mile and record close to 82 mph.' Kimber was increasingly conscious of the low maximum speeds of his bulky sixes, and at this time he tried to ensure that the road-test fleet gave a little more performance than the production examples were capable of offering.

In racing, the company was supreme in its chosen fields. When, in reaction to the over-whelming success achieved by the 750-cc cars, the handicappers clamped down, the company switched to 1,100s. When superchargers were penalized, as in the 1934 TT, out of the hat, it seemed, came the 1,271-cc, 75-bhp NE Magnette. It was the same story in record-breaking, whether it was Eyston or Horton, or even Kohlrausch in central Europe. Eyston's 125 mph in the hour with the K3 and Kohlrausch's 140 mph with EX 127 were headline-making performances and they established MG's name as one of the greatest of racing marques.

But production was pretty well halved from the 1932 peak of 2,400 Midgets, 18/80 and F-types sold, to only some 1,200 sold in 1935. Figures like that added up to a pretty severe cash-flow problem. Kimber had to some extent been protected from harsh commercial reality by his close relationship with Lord Nuffield. Remembering this period, Cousins said: 'Kimber was not liked because he could do more with William Morris than any of the others'.

When the MG factory went under the Morris umbrella in 1935, Kimber had some new bosses in the uneasy hierarchy. Leonard Lord, the lanky production expert who had brought Morris' market share up to 33 per cent in 1935, took a look at Abingdon and said: 'I won't be satisfied until I see 100 cars a week coming out of here'.

Miles Thomas, who would follow Lord as chief executive at Cowley until he was replaced by Panks in 1947, was no lover of motor racing, being given to heavily ironic articles in *The Morris Owner* on the subject in his early days. By 1935, the Cowley production men, with their pressed-steel expertise and the neat if long-stroke 1,292-cc MPJG engine, now with pushrod overhead valves, could reasonably claim that they were beginning to leave Abingdon behind — the advanced features of the R-type 750-cc racer and the prototype sports-touring car derived from it by Enever notwithstanding.

At this time both Lord and Kimber must have been looking hard at the luxury sports-touring market, where MG, Triumph, AC, Riley and Talbot struggled against American imports to establish themselves, but were being outpaced by William Lyons' SS series, keenly priced, glamorous and fast. Within a couple of seasons SS were to have the considerable benefit of moving away from traditional wooden-framed, metal-panelled body construction to all-steel bodies and flow-line production.

Cowley's response to this was the SA 2-Litre, which appeared in October 1935. Although the Morris bosses were promoting a rationalization programme very heavily at the time, there was not a great deal of interchangeability between the new MG and the 18-hp Wolseley/Morris 'Morley' from which it originated. The bodywork, designed by Kimber, was in the latest fashion and was to be built in-house instead of by Carbodies, who had served for so many years. The engine was a modern overhead-valve unit derived from Wolseley's new 18/80 six and the totally conventional half-elliptic sprung chassis was over-slung front and rear. A central cruciform looked after chassis stiffness. Although a synchromesh four-speed gearbox with cranked lever was first specified, the 2-Litre was to go through a long gestation period and find itself with more than one choice of box before production started in earnest.

Much more significant was the announcement of a new Midget early in 1936. It was Cowley's interpretation of the theme, but with the work carried out by men of the calibre of Enever. The tall 1,292-cc MPJG engine mounted on Morris' 'Equipoise' rubber mountings was the major new feature. Just as the P-type had been a little bigger all round than the J, so was the T-type just a little larger than the P. The track was four inches greater, the wheelbase almost seven inches more. The body was four inches wider and each seat cushion was two-and-a-half inches broader.

Since the policy was now against racing, Abingdon had to find indirect methods of supporting the enthusiastic drivers who brought in so much useful publicity, and the team of T-types built for the 1937 trials season were good examples of the policy. The engine's cylinder-head was shaved to bring the compression ratio up from the standard 6.5 to 7.5:1 and the body was panelled in aluminium to save weight. There was a Wolseley gearbox with usefully low first and second gear ratios, which replaced the standard box with its more 'main-road' ratios. The Cream Cracker team began slowly, but eventually went on to take the *Motor Cycling* Team Championship for 1937 — the top award in the trials world — driven by Toulmin, Crawford and Jones who, to meet the letter of the rules laid down by the Morris bosses, were the owners of their cars. The arrangement was that the factory bought them back at the season's end for a previously agreed sum. Another team of T-types was built for the 1938 trials season, and this had a version of the 1,548-cc engine used, in single-carburettor form, in the VA-model MG. This was finally bored to 1,708 cc and the Cream Crackers retained their edge over the competition until war put a stop to the classic trials, such as the Colmore, the Land's End, the Edinburgh and the Exeter.

In May 1939 the first of the TB Midgets with the XPAG engine appeared. At 15½ cwt factory weight (17¼ cwt according to *The Autocar)* it was just a little lighter than the earlier car. The new 1,250-cc engine was still ex-Morris, but the bore was wider and the stroke shorter. In a discursive account of his experiences with one of the last to leave the factory before the war stopped production in 1939, *The Autocar's* Linfield had this to say: 'It would be difficult to find a car of similar liveliness and all-round performance — interesting performance — that would be as economical, and this was with a barely run-in engine that had not had any special settings'.

It was now getting on towards nine years from the troubled years of the slump and the motor industry was beginning to think that it could expand its market for cars such as the Midget. There was a sharp contrast between the original M-type coupe that was only available in black, to the jewel-like colours chosen for the TB. There was still black, but there was also red, blue, maroon or metallic grey, all with matching or contrasting interior colours and the option of duo-tone schemes — the wings being painted in any of the standard colours to choice. The TB was not merely a sports car. It was beginning to find a new market as a second car, for a wife to use or a young son or daughter. No doubt with an understanding that such a market existed, the little two-seater drophead was designed and built by Tickford. The weight was creeping up, but the car's appeal was widened.

Meanwhile, the SA had stumbled into production. It was no lightweight, but was a good example of a peculiarly English type of main-road cruiser. Kimber, presumably having decided that providing slightly tweaked cars for road-test was counter-productive, had instead arranged for *The Motor's* technical editor Laurence Pomeroy Jr. to have one of the 2-Litre dropheads, and in this he covered some 20,000 miles with great enjoyment, reporting on his experiences in 1938.

He certainly liked the MG, remarking that even after road-testing cars of the price bracket of the 4¼-litre Bentley and the Lagonda V12 and returning to the MG, 'with one's critical faculties thoroughly sharpened', he found that nothing was more pleasing than the 2-Litre. Part of the pleasure must have been in the car's reliability. Prewar bodies were nothing like as durable as those of modern cars in terms of paintwork and chromium plating, and work on these parts of the car, plus attention to clutch, shock absorbers and road springs which were showing signs of wear, was required. But a total of £35 covered these points and since only minor adjustments to tappets and the brakes was necessary, his car must have been most reliable by any standards. Oil was used at 1,200 mpg, which would be unacceptable today, and the fuel consumption averaged 16/18 mpg. Altogether he counted running costs of under 2d (0.8p) per mile with tyres that lasted some 25,000 miles.

If such results were in any way characteristic of the type, the struggle for sales between the SS Jaguar 2½-litre and the MG in its later WA 2.6-litre form would have been fierce indeed. But the 2.6 did not appear on the market until late-1938, and with the outbreak of war in 1939 the two vehicles were scarcely to join battle. In any case the Morris engineers had a horse of a different colour up their sleeve.

If motor racing by the factory had been banned by edict, many owners still carried on, the K3 and the Q-type becoming a particular focus for those who would improve on near-perfection. The main object was to reduce the wind-resistance and weight of the standard K3, and the late Series 1 model of J.H.T. Smith was a good example of the intelligent tuner's approach. This car wound up in 1939 with a neat single-seater body on modern GP lines on a chassis that had been lightened and improved in detail with hydraulic brakes, to make it suitable for road races on contemporary circuits such as Donington Park and the Campbell circuit at Brooklands.

The greatest of all K3 specials was an amalgam of the special chassis built for Eyston with an off-set transmission line and a narrow streamlined bodyshell like that of the Magic Midget, plus the ex-Horton offset single-seater K3 which in Gardner's hands took the Brooklands 1,100-cc class lap record at 124.4 mph on Bank Holiday Monday in August 1936.

The following year the German record week saw the Horton car covering the measured mile on the Frankfurt *autobahn* at 148.8 mph in Gardner's hands, and it was during this visit to Germany that the scientifically-inclined Dr Porsche suggested that a more modern envelope for the car would bring considerable benefits.

Barred by the Versailles peace treaty from building high-speed aircraft, the renascent Germans took to Grand Prix racing as a showplace for their technology, entering teams of revolutionary machines from Mercedes-Benz and Auto-Union. Efficiently, they explored the limits of roadholding and engine design on the demanding circuits of Italy, France and elsewhere, and when the season ended they took over sections of ruler-straight *autobahnen*. There, with specially streamlined cars, they investigated with cool precision on the ground similar problems to those Britain had been exploring in the air with the streamlined monoplanes evolved from the Schneider Trophy seaplane racers.

As in the air, progress was rapid. At the end of 1938 a 6-litre Mercedes-Benz had covered the measured-mile at a mean speed of 268.9 mph, aided by full-width wind-cheating bodywork. Records under the well-organized conditions of Germany were clearly a different business from struggling round the jerry-built Brooklands banking or battling with wind and tide on Pendine Sands. There were certainly problems with the wind, and the brilliant young Rosemeyer had been killed in an Auto-Union in gusty conditions, but after Gardner returned from Frankfurt, Kimber's interest was whetted and he persuaded Lord Nuffield that it would be a good idea to sponsor the construction of a suitable record-breaker.

The Germans were helpful, providing Abingdon with co-ordinates and other facts and figures to permit a suitable shell to be created. Reid Railton, already a respected name, who had been at the record week with John Cobb, for whom he had just created the Railton Special land-speed-record car, was commissioned to design the new body. Since the Railton Special was to go faster on less power from its old Napier aero engines than any other land-speed-record car for years afterwards, and the MG's output would be limited, he was a very suitable choice.

The result was a car of quite exceptional beauty and one which has proved difficult to surpass in efficiency, in part due to its narrow tyres, which offered less wind resistance than the fatter ones used by modern record contenders. The driver had to accept a recumbent posture and there were strict limits on the steering and suspension movement, but these were not thought to be significant since the car was intended to run on a straight, smooth surface.

There were ducts to control airflow to the radiators inside the skin, and the windscreen was partially enclosed. The first artist's sketch was released in March 1938 and in June Lord Nuffield gave a party to introduce the Gardner-MG, as it was to be known. Clearly Kimber had relied on the argument that even if the racing cars were not like the production cars, at least the work being done on the new record-breaker would benefit the bread-and-butter car of the future, for his Lordship echoed the argument in his introduction. 'You can't buy anything like the German racing cars,' he pointed out, and the Magnette was much more the sort of thing that could be bought. 'It has, for instance, a number of standard parts and is basically a production model.' The production model, of course, was the K3, and the last of the 31 built had left the works in 1934.

Gardner's first outing in the new car was on the Frankfurt-Dessau *autobahn* in 1938, where he turned in a stunning 187.6 mph average. It was a measure of the car's superiority that its speed was greater than the records for the 1½ and 3-litre classes (both held by Maseratis). The MG managed its performance on only 194 bhp, while the Mercedes-Benz had called upon 600 bhp to force its clean but bulky form and vast tyres up to 268 mph. The lesson was certainly 'keep it small'. The Hawker Fury biplane fighter of the RAF in the early-1930s needed 530 bhp from its Kestrel engine for 207 mph, but the tiny Mew Gull, the smallest airframe that could be devised to carry the Gipsy

Six engine and a pilot into the air, managed 255 mph from 230 bhp in 1936.

As Baron von Falkenhausen told guests at a BARC dinner at the Dorchester Hotel in London: 'After the record quite a number of people were running about like so many chickens exclaiming, "amazing, unbelievable!".' It was no surprise that in 1939 the team made their way back to Germany to the Dessau *autobahn*, specially built for record-breaking, with over 200 mph in mind. The engine, by dint of higher blower pressures and much sophisticated attention to detail, was now giving over 200 bhp, which made it the most highly efficient unit of its era, with 185.8 bhp per litre.

The car made two runs to average 203.5 mph with commendable economy of effort. EX 135 was now the first 1,100-cc car to exceed 120 mph, 150 mph and 200 mph. Using a portable boring outfit, Enever and Jackson then enlarged the MG to bring it just into the 1,500-cc class, and their overnight efforts were rewarded when Gardner recorded 204.2 mph. This figure was eventually to be surpassed by EX 181, but the 1,100-cc class figures still stand.

Because of Gardner's considerable height, it had been necessary to extend the car by six inches from its optimum length and possibly because the car was that much longer than theoretically desirable, it was going rather faster than the figures anticipated. 'We were told with 180 bhp we'd get 180 mph. But they were wrong; by getting 190 bhp we got 200 mph,' said Cousins.

At Cowley they were getting on with a new generation of family saloons. The rationalization programme had led to the death of all the overhead-camshaft engines on Morris cars by the summer of 1936, and by 1937 the only side-valve engine was in the Morris Eight. Although they had kept separate chassis-frames until 1939, they were increasingly inclined to attach the body structure to the chassis to make a rigid structure. With the 1939 Ten-Four Series M they introduced full unitary-construction and dropped the separate chassis. As yet the disparagingly titled 'Tin Ten' was no lightweight, but the structure was stiff enough to benefit from independent front suspension. By 1938 the results of Olley's researches at General Motors had been digested in Britain and the Ten had unequal-length wishbones with coil springs at the front when it was built as a prototype. At the time, chassis and suspension engineers of the calibre of Boyle, Daniels, Issigonis and Charles were working for Morris, and when at last it was decided that the world was not ready for Morris IFS, they took the enterprising step of making the production leaf-springs of the rigid front axle much softer than those of the back, with a roll-bar at the front axle designed by Charles. The end result was a most satisfactory medium-sized family car with much-above-average handling.

There was also to be an MG Ten with IFS and rack-and-pinion steering. It was a neat little saloon, with body panels like those of the Morris Eight Series E and a separate chassis like that of the Eight, but as with the Wolseley Ten it resembled so closely, war intervened and production was prevented until after the hostilities were over. It seems likely that if production had continued through 1940 and 1941, this little car would have been found preferable by many people to Kimber's own impressive six-cylinder WA 2.6-Litre.

But by 1941, Kimber, showing an intransigence that had increasingly soured his relations with his Morris bosses, had fallen out with Miles Thomas over war work and munitions contracts and had left the company he had formed and shaped so resolutely. He died in 1945, the victim of what had otherwise seemed to be a rather minor train accident in London.

CHAPTER FIVE

The Midgets — into world markets

The war years were a long hard slog for the Abingdon workforce, as for so many others. A number of designers in the motor industry sought relief from the pressures by scheming-out pipe dreams, and some of these, such as Heynes' twin-overhead-camshaft Jaguar engine and Issigonis' 'Mosquito' small saloon, were to find their way into production. Sadly, no such pipe dreams were brought to life at Abingdon. Everybody concerned with the prewar Midget knew it was outdated even when the TA came out in 1936, and there were plenty of pointers to the way design could go. In 1934 a 58 x 94 mm 1,500-cc BMW six won the team prize in the Alpine Trial. It went into production as a 50-bhp two-seater with IFS and a 4:1 rear-axle ratio, weighing only about 15 cwt. The Fiat 508C was an 1,100-cc four with short-stroke dimensions of 68 x 75 mm and pushrod overhead valves that showed itself to have great tuning potential.

But when the Midget went back into production as the TC the engine was the same long-stroke unit and the only substantial mechanical change was the substitution of swinging spring shackles for the trunnions that had so long been the Midget's unique characteristic. It was a change brought about after an examination of service records had shown that this was the most troublesome feature in the car. 'It was a shame, really,' said Cousins, 'it was the only thing left that was truly MG.' The other change was to make the body wider; the seat squab now measured a comfortable four inches more across and was a little higher. Production was under way by October 1945. In those austere postwar years, cars were usually painted severe black, and this was the colour that Miles Thomas had decreed for the MG, as the 1946 buyers' guides confirm. But after a few months Cousins, as works manager, felt this was just not good enough. 'Being a bit of a rebel, I said, "you can't sell black sports cars". So the first batch of cars — an order for 20 or 25 — were painted five in blue, five in red, five in green and so on. They all went to Nuffield Export, out of my control. Miles Thomas saw those pretty cars going down the road in colours we hadn't seen since before the war. He had me up on the carpet, but I made the excuse that those were our prewar colours and he let it pass.'

The decision to stay with the ex-Morris XPAG 1,250-cc engine in the TC was to have important implications in the postwar era, for although it was still of overly long stroke, it was in the mainstream of European engine technology, which was increasingly focussed on the small OHV four, and it was thus able to benefit from improvements in lubricants and in materials technology for its bearings.

The man who did so much to direct and guide the MG company's fortunes in the postwar period was John Thornley, who joined in November 1931 in the service department, with the additional task of setting up the MG Car Club, which was then just beginning to get under way. In due course he became service manager, but as an enthusiastic MG owner and driver he became involved in many other activities too, and on his return after the war he became director and general manager. It was to him that the task of keeping the company's name in the mind of sports-car owners devolved. With a basically unsympathetic upper echelon to deal with Thornley often found himself joining with other MG executives in strategems in order to help the new generation of competition drivers to be competitive with the ever-improving opposition. To Thornley, too, must go much of the credit for understanding just how important the international markets overseas, and particularly in North America, were to become.

The Collier brothers, wealthy heirs to a New York advertising agency, had imported a few MGs before the war, coming to an agreement with Abingdon in 1934 to set up an American distributorship based in Long Island, New York. The Colliers were instrumental in establishing the Automobile Racing Club of America, which organized race meetings on the general lines of European road-racing on an increasingly ambitious scale through the late-1930s. Many MGs competed in these events, with J2s prominent, although Miles Collier built a very effective special with an aluminium racing body which anticipated postwar specials such as the Lester MG. The Collier was based on one of the 1935 Le Mans PA Midgets, equipped with a Marshall blower and with the rear-axle ratio raised by the use of the NE crownwheel-and-pinion. The special was brought to Le Mans in 1939 and ran consistently until the ninth hour, when a burst fuel tank caused its retirement.

The postwar impact of the MG in the USA was summed-up neatly by John Bond in *Road & Track* in 1963. 'The fabulous MG TC invaded America in 1948 and as we all know, started the revolution. It couldn't climb a 6 per cent grade in top gear, its honest top speed was under 80 mph and it rode like a Model A Ford. But despite this it was a tremendous success for one very good reason — it brought back driving enjoyment.'

As the USA market grew larger a more effective sales network was developed. The Hambro Trading Company of America became sole concessionaires and distributors such as International Motors, British Motor Car Company, Inskip, and Waco Motors started operating from Los Angeles, San Francisco, Dallas, New York and Miami. 'The most famous sportscar in the world. Finest British craftsmanship, smart appearance and faultless performance have won for this thoroughbred an unrivalled reputation. A small car masterpiece for the connoisseur', was the way that Inskip worded their advertisements for the TC.

By the time *The Autocar* tested the TC in October 1947 even the British were beginning to realize that independent front suspension was here to stay, and the journal's report is coloured by their awareness. 'Merits and demerits of normal-versus-independent suspension can be argued . . . The normally sprung car, rather hard sprung as in this instance, does let the driver gauge within close limits the speeds at which he can corner fast.' They found that the Midget was no more difficult to drive than a family saloon, but if the gearbox is used, '. . . the performance becomes quite vivid'.

The previous spring had seen the announcement of the MG Ten at last, but now, since the old RAC hp ratings were no longer appropriate, it was called the 1¼-Litre. Like the prewar project, it featured IFS and rack-and-pinion steering. This Y-type saloon was just what the depressed English middle-classes wanted in the postwar austerity years, and it sold briskly, acquiring some unexpectedly devoted followers when owners realized how well it could be persuaded to go. There was a somewhat lighter tourer from 1948, but the greatest importance of the plushly equipped little saloon, with its leather seats, polished woodwork and generously dimensioned sliding roof, lay in what was developed from it.

Cousins and Enever were desperate to take the TC design out of the stagnant backwater it occupied at Abingdon. Enever had yet more ambitious thoughts, but the Nuffield management were not at all keen to see improvements made. The weaknesses of the old-fashioned chassis were highlighted by the power that could now be extracted from the enthusiastic owner who followed Abingdon's tuning manual, schemed out by Enever and the first of its kind, and by the problems that were revealed when the team of TCs was entered for the first of the *Daily Express* production car races at Silverstone. As Dick Jacobs has related, until fairly drastic action was taken over wheels and tyres, springs and shock absorbers, the cars were woefully uncompetitive against well-prepared HRG 1500 two-seaters.

By this time, the TC's sales were beginning to slip, particularly in the USA. Cousins recalls: 'There was S. V. Smith, who wasn't all that wrapped up in us, with the technical director Vic Oak. He came to see us once a week on Tuesday mornings. We told him we wanted IFS and he said he'd see about it. So we took a Y-type, cut five inches out, put in a gusset, turned it over and joined it up. We had put a T-type body on it by the time he came over the next week and we showed him. The thing was broken-backed. He said, "I'm going on holiday. I'll be back in a fortnight and I want to see this motor in a fit state".'

They built the TD in a fortnight as required and Cousins recalled: 'I drove it to Marcham myself to make sure it worked. It took them 12 months to copy it in the drawing office and put it in

production'.

In fact the TD was announced in early 1950, having started production late in 1949. The now familiar Y-type rack-and-pinion steering and coil-spring IFS was installed in a derivative of the same car's chassis, but the rear-end passed over the rear axle. The engine was the same XPAG 1,250 twin-carburettor unit, but the gearbox had the wider ratios of the Y-type. The wheels were now 15-inch discs which in effect reduced the overall gear ratio; mph per 1,000 rpm was 14.5 against the 15.5 mph per 1,000 of the TC. The body was again wider by four inches and the interior was generally a little more spacious everywhere than the TC had been. Softer springs meant a more gentle ride for the TD. Once again the enthusiasts were initially unimpressed by the car, but the more objective of the motoring press testers persuaded them to give it the favourable response that it was to earn in its major markets overseas.

Purchased in their thousands by keen drivers all over the world, the TC and TD Midgets saw service in every possible form of motoring competition. Although in standard form they were never competitive in international events, they could be tuned, and the factory's tuning manual showed exactly how it should be done without the expensive disasters that too often could follow over-enthusiastic work by amateurs. Tuning in stages, the engine could give up to 83 bhp at 6,000 rpm or 97 bhp with a low-pressure blower.

In the early postwar days the TC was good enough to take on the best in the Alpine Rally, and Betty Haig won the 1,500-cc class in the 1949 event against tough opposition provided by the HRG team. In the Alpine the following year two teams of Midgets performed with distinction; Swiss owners Kenk and Keller won the 1,500-cc class with TD Midgets and with de Rebibus won the Foreign Team Trophy, leading home the cars of Flower (TD), Cunane and Laramie (TCs).

Road-testers invariably had kind words to write about MG Midgets as each successive new model passed through their hands — even though there were veiled comments about the harsh ride of the pre-IFS models — and when the TD was tested by *The Autocar* in 1953 they were glowing. 'The high-geared rack-and-pinion steering is light, accurate and responsive and small movements of the wheel produce a quick response. On the open road it is necessary to hold the wheel only lightly and long fast bends are taken more by leaning the body into the corner than by steering round it.' Once upon a time that kind of accolade was given only to costly continental thoroughbreds such as the Alfa Romeo 1750 or the Bugatti type 43.

This test was illuminating on speeds. '. . . 65 mph (is) reached easily, and a cruising speed of 60-65 mph can be maintained whenever conditions allow. Above these figures however the increase is slower and to reach 75 mph on the slightly flattering speedometer requires a fair length of road. With the windscreen flat and only the driver in the car a true speed of 78 mph was reached on level ground on two occasions.' Certainly the old saying that the Midget needed 100 hp for 100 mph was borne out in practice.

By this time Abingdon knew very well what needed to be done. It was time for a modern all-enveloping roadster to be produced. The special-bodied TD built for George Phillips to drive in the 1951 Le Mans 24-hours race showed what Enever had in mind, and one Abingdon executive wrote on returning from a visit to the USA, '. . . the Midget is underpowered . . . The engine is working too hard at their cruising speeds and distances. Excessive weight of TD causes comment. There is great scope for future MG sales. But the cars have got to keep up with the times, be exceptional in style,'.

His recommendation was to revamp the TD with a new body, to offer a 1,500-cc engine with a 2,700-cc unit as an option. He also thought that a lightweight MG road-racing car was needed. 'Sell them a car capable of making a good showing and let the owners do the racing.' But nobody at Nuffield was really listening. Other projects from other factories were preferred in 1952.

What actually came along in October 1954 — 'Sweeter and lower than ever before', said the publicity — was the TF, which was very good in its way but not the modern high-speed item that Abingdon really needed and knew exactly how to make. They knew it, too, at Nuffield for nobody on the UK journals seems to have tested one fully in totally standard form, with the later 1,500 engine. No doubt it would have been faster than the TD, for the overall height was down by 1½ inches and even in 1,250-cc form it was sold in what amounted to stage-two tune — 57 bhp at 5,500 rpm, with larger valves and stronger springs as well as larger SU carburettors.

But by 1953 there were some cheap, and there were some pretty, 100-mph two-seaters on the market; Triumph's TR2, Austin-Healey's 100 and AC's Ace were all of at least 2-litres swept volume, and all had great development potential. It must have been galling for Thornley, Cousins, Enever and their team to see such an enormous gap opening up in the market when they knew they had the very car that would fit and they weren't allowed to build it.

CHAPTER SIX

The cast-iron investments

When Nuffield and Austin amalgamated to create the British Motor Corporation one of the first fruits for MG was a tidy four-cylinder pushrod overhead-valve engine of 1,489 cc. The new engine was to become famous as the B-series unit which, in different forms, was to power several generations of BMC cars and their successors over the next two decades. In the process it was to appear in a variety of swept volumes from the original 1,200-cc unit, installed in the postwar Austin A40, to the 2,004-cc version in a specially prepared stopgap MGB GT used at Sebring when the MGC had not been homologated in time. The B-series' antecedents were prewar, when an Austin 10-hp side-valve engine was modified to take the rolled steel-backed babbitt metal crankshaft and big-end bearings imported by G.A. Vandervell from America. In 1946 Austin's 12-hp engine was still fitted with side valves, but there was a water pump and thermostat to replace the earlier thermosyphon arrangement. Side valves in the cylinder-block produced distortion, and head design limited the compression ratio to 7:1, so the next move was to put the valves in the head, at which point the 65.5 × 88.9 mm unit gave 39 bhp.

In the 1,200-cc A40 Devon the power was said to be 42 bhp at 4,300 rpm. The induction and exhaust assemblies were located on the opposite side of the block to the electrical equipment, and the pushrods passed through passages on the induction side of the head to avoid the need to use tubes to cross the plug recesses. A forged crankshaft was carried on three bearings and the connecting-rods were split at an angle to make it possible to withdraw them through the bores. The crank and rods were forged in 50-ton rather than 40-ton steel to keep the assembly smaller and reduce its weight. The 1,489-cc version of the engine was bored to 73 mm, the stroke remaining unchanged, and in the MG version it was fitted with twin SU carburettors, double valve springs and a large-valve cylinder-head. Another innovation was copper/lead alloy for the big-ends to withstand the greater loadings.

To ensure consistent oil consumption throughout the large-scale production runs envisaged for the B-series unit, four rings were fitted to the pistons. A chrome top ring was introduced later and bore life was doubled since it could better resist the corrosion effects of the products of combustion. Rather than honing, the cylinders were bored with a single-point tool to produce a fine thread-like finish, wire-brushed and finally rolled, the object being to produce a finish which, less than mirror-like, was coarse enough to retain a film of oil. The object was achieved, with a bore life in excess of 80,000 miles often resulting in minimal wear. A most extensive source of trouble in immediate prewar engines was piston seizure, and this was cured, on the aluminium pistons, by careful tailoring of the piston shape to suit the temperature gradient and by the use of split skirts with low-expansion alloys.

In one of those sad little ironies that abound in the later years of the MG story, while the determinedly traditionalist TF was being prepared for its short production life, the best small MG saloon yet was also ready to be launched in October 1953 and was as modern as could be wished. Like the 1,489-cc B-series engine which powered it with a willing 60 bhp, the Magnette ZA was a BMC product, a badge-engineered variant of the Wolseley 4/44. There was a shapely unitary-construction hull to provide a robust substructure for the by now customary wishbone-and-coil-spring suspension at the front and the conventional leaf springs supporting a live axle at the rear. To control axle movement there was a torque-arm firmly bolted to the rear-axle casing and pivoting at its front on a central body cross-member. The MG advertisement at the time spoke about, 'The beauty of airsmoothed styling,' and it was evident that the restrained lines had been influenced by such cars as Pininfarina's Lancia Aurelia B20 GT. A full complement of four well-upholstered and leather-covered seats was provided, plus plenty of polished woodwork.

None of this saved the Magnette from outraged comment in the motoring journals about 'the abuse' of the honoured title, but this little saloon is one MG that has kept its appeal down the years. It was a doughty performer in competitions, too, always showing well in the saloon car events that were so popular in British racing at the time, and winning the Saloon Car Championship in 1958.

The benefits of the Magnette's monocoque construction were evident. It had 60 bhp and

weighed 22 cwt in road-test form against the 21 cwt and 46 bhp of the 1¼-litre saloon. Add to that the benefits of the all-enveloping shell and the Z-series looks a genuine step forward. One tester certainly thought it was. 'The MG Magnette is one of the finer cars *The Autocar* has tested. It is extremely comfortable, good looking and safe.' Wet or dry roads made no difference to its performance, and under appallingly wet conditions, the Magnette negotiated a right-hand corner which formed part of the private test circuit at a higher speed than any car the tester had driven through there in rain or shine.

In the postwar years there had been little official support from the factory management for motor racing, despite their enthusiasm. John Thornley and Syd Enever helped almost secretly when an owner came along with a worthwhile project, but were only able to come out in the open with record-breaking when Gardner revived EX 135 and drove it with a variety of engines ranging in capacity from 350 to 1,500 cc. He managed 121 mph with the prewar six-cylinder engine running as a 350-cc twin and in August 1952 used this effective record-breaker, powered by a blown version of the TD engine, to set records at up to more than 189 mph, despite having spun the car at 150 mph and sustained minor injuries when he collided with a marker four days earlier.

Then in 1954 the company built a new record-breaker specifically to attack American 1,500 cc-class records. EX 179 looked not unlike its great predecessor, but was shorter and used an important prototype chassis-frame. Into this efficient structure was fitted a 1,500-cc version of the 1,250-cc TD engine, driving through a standard gearbox to a special rear axle with a choice of ratios up to 2.9:1. Driven by Eyston and Miles, the car set 35 records, from 10 miles to 12 hours, at 118.7 mph to 153.7 mph. Abingdon had good cause to feel pleased, since the chassis was one of those schemed out by Enever for the forthcoming MGA.

The second driver on this attack, the celebrated Ken Miles, built a pair of MG specials that have gone down in the mythology of the USA racing scene. His first special used a modified TD Mark II engine and from the first outing at Pebble Beach in 1953 it was a winner. Miles established himself as the West Coast's finest small-car driver, and with his second MG, the Flying Shingle (roof slate) — so called for its low build — which had a modified TF engine and a TC gearbox, he went on to a remarkable series of giant-killing performances. Miles also drove a more standard-looking TF during most of 1954, and it must be very much due to his performances with these cars that American enthusiasts realized just how raceworthy were the 'outmoded' T-series cars. Midgets were campaigned in the USA long after the British had decided there was no hope for them. It was a pattern that was to be repeated again in the 1970s, over 20 years later.

MG production had fallen back from a 1952 peak of 12,000 cars to less than 9,000 in the following year. In 1954 production began to pick up again, but despite the ready acceptance of the TD in overseas markets it was the saloon cars which were providing an increasing proportion of sales. At last the Nuffield management relented, and allowed Enever his head to produce the modern two-seater he had had standing ready virtually since that special-bodied TD he built for the 1951 Le Mans race.

There were at least two of these new chassis-frames in existence. One of them was used for EX 179, the TD-engined record-breaker, and another was the basis of a sports two-seater called EX 175. It was quite a massive structure, built up from box-section members and partly triangulated at the front. The rear-end swept over the axle, which was suspended on conventional half-elliptics. At the front it was all very familiar, with the wishbone suspension and rack-and-pinion steering mounted on a very substantial subframe. The first of these new cars was equipped with the TF's long-stroke engine, which resulted in the unique small bulge in the bonnet.

The next stage was the team of Le Mans cars built for the 1955 race. As chief engineer, Enever's brief was to stay close to the as yet unannounced production model, the new MGA; this he did, but characteristically the team cars were meticulously prepared. There was a full light-alloy underpan and low drag figures were claimed. Cylinder-head changes designed by Weslake brought the power up to 82 bhp and the total weight in race trim was 14½ cwt, thanks to light-alloy panelling held to the body-frame by countersunk rivets.

With a curved aero screen and the second seat faired over the team cars were good for 94 mph laps and in the tragedy-filled Le Mans race of 1955 they showed well, with 119 mph being recorded through the kilometre trap on the Mulsanne straight, using a 3.7:1 rear axle. After the event the cars were given 4.3:1 axles for the Alpine Rally, and then they were entered in the Tourist Trophy at Dundrod. The Le Mans cars were made available to the press during the summer of 1955 and proved to be thoroughly satisfactory road-going cars. Testers liked the new seating position — in the modern manner the seat was further from the wheel than in the T-series — the suspension and roadholding were judged to be of a very high order, the Lockheed brakes were superb, and the gearchange was liked, although there were reservations about the widely spaced ratios.

In summary, the tester from *The Autocar* said, 'If the engine can be offered without too much detuning and the weight kept down to the present level, this delightful car will be a serious contender in the small high-performance class.'

Autosport's John Bolster certainly enjoyed himself with the car, '. . . on a road circuit I allowed myself to take some corners on full throttle in third gear at an extreme angle of drift. Few normal sports cars would remain completely under control when handled in such an uninhibited manner.'

By the following September the first production models were rolling out of Abingdon. The name Midget was dropped and MGA became the chosen title. The response from enthusiasts and press was uniformly good — probably better than any MG had received since the PB of 20 years before. Of course the engine power *was* less at 68 bhp and the weight *had* gone up to 18¼ cwt, but the car was intended to appeal to a much wider market than MG sports models had been able to in the past. There was a new market for the sporting but comfortable car in the USA, and a similar market was to grow in Europe as times became more prosperous. It was a market that the MGA was well schemed to exploit, for with a top speed in road-test form of 97.8 mph and a standing-quarter-mile time of 20 seconds there was plenty of performance. The only possible difficulty was that the car looked as big as the Triumph TR sports of 2 litres and the Austin-Healey of 2.4 litres, yet since it was of only 1½ litres it could not match them on performance, while the light and high-geared Triumph TR2 was a remarkably economical car, recording 32-34 mpg overall on test against the MGA's 26.7 mpg.

It was obvious that more power was needed, and from the very beginning in 1956 a larger-sized, twin-overhead-camshaft version of the B-series engine had been planned for the MGA. In the 1955 TT two of the EX 182 cars had twin-ohc engines, one designed by Longbridge, one by Abingdon.

In purely engineering terms the Twin Cam engine was a fine design, and when it was installed

29

in a new record-breaker it was destined to become the fastest engine ever built by the factory. EX 181 was a successful attempt to improve on the near-perfection of the closely related shapes of EX 135 and 179, and Enever kept to certain basic principles embodied in the earlier cars while introducing new ideas to improve the car's usefulness and performance. Most important, as for the earlier cars the aerofoil shape was given a slight negative angle of incidence to ensure that the car's passage through the air did not generate lift. There were most carefully calculated rear contours to control airflow, and the oval cross-section of the shell made it possible to use standard IFS with plenty of steering and suspension movement without recourse to any energy-consuming bulges or other aerodynamic compromises.

EX 181 made two successful sorties to Utah, finally setting 2-litre international class records at over 254 mph in 1959 driven by Phil Hill.

When, after a very long period of development, the Twin Cam was finally released into production in 1958, it transformed the MGA. All the power the car needed was available at last, and with 108 bhp on tap the maximum speed went up to 114 mph, although the 18.6 seconds taken for the standing-quarter-mile reflected a kerb weight now up to 19¼ cwt; one road-tester felt that the ratios were still too widely spaced and closer ratios were introduced later.

Although the car was welcomed in this form there were some ominous comments, with testers disliking a '. . . constant, rather obtrusive back-ground of mechanical noise . . .' (The Autocar), and commenting on an oil consumption of one pint for every 120 miles (The Motor). In general driving the car was tractable and with the revised front springs allied to slightly stronger shock absorbers, the ride was tighter — cornering power was held to be greater. Regrettably, few contemporary observers had the grasp of Road & Track, which realized that, 'designed primarily to regain prestige for the marque in production sports-car racing, it should do just that'. The Twin Cam was in fact the realization of that management recommendation of the T-series days — 'Sell them a car capable of making a showing and let the owners do the racing'.

Sadly, its price and ready availability — 750 a year were planned — meant that it found its way into the hands of owners without the necessary mechanical sympathy to use the Twin Cam properly, and after only two years a host of maintenance problems led to the withdrawal of the model. The demise of this superb unit, mourned by many, was less disastrous than it might have been, for a bigger, more powerful version of the ever-willing pushrod OHV B-series engine was introduced in 1959.

The 1,588-cc MGA 1600 was bored-out from the earlier engine. There was a small increase in power, but more important was the torque offered by the bigger unit. It meant there were considerable improvements in the mid-range acceleration figures, with a second saved from the third-gear 40-60 mph time and 2.8 seconds from the same speed range in top. Top speed was no more than before, but as The Motor's tester explained, what mattered was the ease and rapidity with which 80 mph could be reached and maintained whenever there was a slight break in the traffic on ordinary main roads. 'The car's speed — with the moral and physical support of superlative brakes — was the speed of the road,' said another man from The Motor.

Another 1600 came along in 1961, but this was much more than the previous straight-forward stretching of the B-series unit. With an eye on making it still bigger in the future, the engine was largely reworked and came out at 1,622 cc, the cylinder-block being redesigned with siamesed bores to enable the machine lines to open-out the cylinders to 75.4 mm. As had been the case when enormous strides in power outputs were made by Abingdon in the early-1930s with highly boosted racing engines, materials technology and lubrication were at the root of this latest improvement. Power was now well over twice the original at 83 bhp, delivered at 5,600 rpm, and BMC engineers readily admitted it was possible largely because of the use of much-improved bearing materials, in this case Vandervell VP3. A new cylinder-head, with still bigger valves, was matched by a new crankshaft, connecting-rods and pistons. Full-flow oil filtration was now essential because hard particles could not embed themselves harmlessly into the copper-lead bearing material as they could in white metal.

With this engine it was at last possible for the MGA to exceed 100 mph without help from wind or gradient. The great heyday of the BMC works rally teams was just beginning under the brilliant leadership of Marcus Chambers, who had to weld a convincing unit from the disparate elements that were available to him from the motley range the Corporation offered at the time. The teams were based at Abingdon and it was there that the soon to be world-famous group of development engineers and racing mechanics prepared, to magnificent effect, the MGAs, Austin-Healeys and Minis which won so many championships under Chambers, then Turner and later Browning. Although the MGA was not to be a major team car, the Ladies' Rally Championships of 1956 and 1957 were won by Nancy Mitchell using an MGA for part of the season, while it took the *Autosport* Production Sports Car Championship in 1956.

The TC had prepared the way in the important American market, the TD took Abingdon into large-scale sales, but it was the MGA's great achievement to become a big-league sports car, in terms of acceptance by enthusiasts around the world and for its sales — 101,000-plus by the time production ceased — before giving way to another generation of MG sports cars, in 1962.

CHAPTER SEVEN

Unitary construction

Although it had been so ungenerously greeted on its arrival, the Z-series Magnette went on to create quite a devoted following for itself. By the time it went out of production in late-1958 it was beginning to look rather heavy, for unitary construction methods were improving and bodies were becoming lighter without loss of strength. The Magnette had received its share of benefits from the improvements to the B-series engine and by the summer of 1958 it was provided with 69 bhp. *Autosport* considered it the best car of the BMC range, saying that although it had no advanced features and was of conservative appearance, it was a well made car which had been developed to a point where it could hold its own with vehicles of more modern conception.

But in due course it left the scene, to be replaced by the Magnette Mark III, a product of a new rationalization programme which was not built at Abingdon at all, but came down the BMC lines with its pretty well identical twin, the Morris Oxford. Although its performance was little different from that of the Z-series, its origins betrayed it and its manner of going was in no way to be compared with that of any other MG.

Also in a sense a badge-engineered car, the MG Midget was introduced in June 1961. It was developed from the Austin-Healey Sprite which first appeared in May 1958 and shared with it the willing little A-series engine and Austin A35-based

gearbox, as well as the front suspension to which was mated the Morris Minor rack-and-pinion steering. It, too, was of full unitary construction, and at 948 cc it was the smallest MG since the P-series Midget of the mid-1930s. But this Midget had a 9.1:1 compression ratio, twin SU carburettors of 1¼-inch bore and gave 49.8 bhp. There was a usefully close set of gearbox ratios, and the Midget settled down to a brisk demand.

Although it was derived from the Austin-Healey, and indeed was produced simultaneously with identical cars labelled Sprite, the ADO 47 Midget was very much an Abingdon project. There is a story that Syd Enever was asked to style the new car's rear-half while the front-end was altered at the Warwick headquarters of Austin-Healey, and that the two ends had to be worked on quite independently. Certainly the Sprite Mark II H-AN6-cum-Midget Mark I G-AN1 bodyshell from the windscreen aft bore a strong resemblance to the Mini-based ADO 34 two-seater sports project that Abingdon dearly wanted to build. Fitted out with comfortable bucket seats, adequate instruments and metal-framed detachable sidescreens, the Midget was modestly priced at £641 basic — less some items of equipment, such as bumpers, that might be thought to be fairly essential.

Modest though they were, those first Midgets made an immediate impression. Despite the tiny engine they accelerated like no Midget had ever done before, and with the tight quarter-elliptic rear suspension they cornered flat and fast, but front disc brakes were needed to provide stopping power in keeping. Towards the end of 1962 the engine went up to 1,098 cc, in which form it eventually gave some 59 bhp at 5,250 rpm, but it was still only in the early stages of what was to be a long career.

It had begun at Longbridge in 1949 when, freed from the old RAC formula taxation scheme which favoured long strokes and was largely responsible for the tall format of the XPAG unit, Appleby and Oak brought out a new engine with a 58 mm bore and 76.2 mm stroke giving 803 cc. Historically the dimensions were close to the beloved old Austin Seven's, but the resemblance ended there. With a quite enterprising 7.2:1 compression ratio the new engine gave 28 bhp, enough to make the original A30 Austin quite a lively baby. The celebrated Harry Weslake had been called in, and he provided Austin with a smaller-scale version of his 'heart-shaped' combustion chamber first seen on the A40 Austin's B-series unit in 1947. With attention to detail in the porting to overcome the inherent disadvantages of the siamesed ports, the A-series engine turned out to be the sort that thrived on tuning.

When *Motor Sport* tested one of the 1,098-cc Midgets in April 1963 it was in 55-bhp form, and the report was enthusiastic. 'The suspension is quite firm, as sudden shocks at the steering wheel and momentary deflection from a straight course convey, but it is notably comfortable for this type of car. Roll is absent, cornering virtually neutral, tail slides can be checked quickly with positive rack-and-pinion steering. This is geared 2½ turns lock to lock and has a useful, never fierce, castor-return action. The brakes are light, powerful and vice-free except for very occasional rubbing sounds from the pads.'

Weighing 13½ cwt kerb weight, the Midget recorded a quarter-mile time of 20.1 seconds, and gave an overall fuel consumption of 39.2 mpg. 'W.B.' was prepared to forgive what he described as a certain outdated crudity in its minor details; it was the best Midget yet, a small sports car at one with its driver, and it was enormous fun.

Late in 1962 two more new MG models appeared. For the first of these, MG's advertising, now masterminded from Sales Division at Longbridge, verged on the hysterical. 'You sly old fox, you! Trust you to have your bread buttered on both sides. Enjoy the most exciting thing that ever happened to family motoring — and still be dashingly different. All right, be smug! So you've got MG pace and verve . . . limousine comfort . . . Hydrolastic smooth ride. You've got everything! Bully for sporty, comfort-loving nonconformist you? MG 1100 from £755.' And so on.

What our smug sporty nonconformist actually got was a badge-engineered twin-carburettor version of BMC's consistently best-selling transverse-engined 1100/1300 model. It was, of course, a delightful little family car offering space and handling much in excess of any of its competitors', and when it was equipped with the ample leather-covered seats and the nicely finished walnut veneer of the MG variant, ADO 16 was a highly refined machine that stayed in brisk demand, but never came near Abingdon during a production life which lasted into the 1970s.

Although the car was low-slung, the driver sat high and benefitted from the coupled Hydrolastic suspension which provided a comparatively pitch-free ride at the expense of some sharp up-and-down motion; Issigonis was responsible with Moulton for the suspension and he also designed the new baulk-ring-type synchromesh for the gearbox. In *Motor Sport's* report they said: 'The fact remains that the MG 1100 can be cornered extremely fast, as on a race circuit, with no vices and complete safety. Normally the steering is almost completely neutral, but ultimately almost uniform understeer causes the car to slide outwards.' With a weight of only 16½ cwt fully equipped, the car showed just what strides the body designers were making in unitary construction.

There was nothing of the badge engineer about the new B-series-engined sports car when it made its bow in 1962. The original concept was of an MGA replacement, taking the existing 1,622-cc engine and MGA underframe with its complete suspension, but using a completely new bodyshell. It was to be styled on lines reminiscent of the raindrop-shaped record-breaker EX 181. Two projects were evaluated at various periods of the MGA's life when a replacement was being considered. A light tubular chassis and light-alloy bodywork similar to that of the 1955 racer EX 182 was fitted to EX 183, while EX 186 was a standard MGA chassis clad in a sleek sports-racing shell and with de Dion rear suspension inserted. Since both cars were intended for long-distance racing of the Le Mans and Sebring type, the bodies were carefully studied in tests at what is now BAC's wind tunnel at Baginton airfield near Coventry. Another appropriate project was the Frua styling exercise, EX 214, which contributed to the interior design of the MGA's successor. The project number for the B was EX 205, and the design went through many stages while the engineers, led by Enever and including Hayter, O'Neill, Brocklehurst, Mitchell and Hounslow, refined their first clumsy, over-long, over-wide and heavy ideas.

After considerable work on body shapes, first with quarter-scale models and then with full-size wooden mock-ups, a new approach was decided upon. What was needed, they concluded, was a completely new design, of monocoque construction, with a shorter wheelbase and overall body length. Rear suspension used a live axle located by parallel trailing-arms and a Panhard rod, with coil springing and hydraulic dampers. Front suspension was by wishbones and coil springs with lever-arm dampers. The steering rack was mounted at the front and the whole assembly was carried on a cross-member bolted to the main frame. A hand-made prototype was built to this specification and considerable road and *pavé* testing was carried out.

The final pre-production MGB was developed from this, but reverted to semi-elliptic springs at the rear with the spring axis inclined forward to give an oversteer condition on roll. The front suspension castor angle was modified to 4 degrees but was otherwise unchanged. At this stage investigations into alternative power units were being made, including a 60-degrees V-4 as well as 2 to 2½-litre fours and sixes, with the object of getting more power into the vehicle.

Since at that time the BMC C-series six-cylinder engine, as used in the Austin-Healey 100 Six and 3000, was available a very early predecessor of the ill-fated MGC series must have been considered in 1961 or before. In the end, the good old B-series engine was chosen because it could be stretched out to 1,800 cc, at which capacity it was anticipated to give 94 bhp on a 8.8:1 compression ratio. The hand-made prototype bodies were built at Morris Motors Bodies Branch in Coventry and the production engineering was put in hand at Swindon in the Pressed Steel Fisher plant.

The monocoque structure of the MGB meant that, at 17 cwt, kerb weight was down despite the provision of far more creature comforts than the A-series had been able to offer. The car was easier to enter and leave because the doors were larger, and the new wind-up windows were matched by a carefully schemed hood to ensure that the rain stayed out even at the 100 mph-plus speed that was now within the province of the car. The seats were more elaborate, with adjustable backs, and there was considerably more interior space. There was a bigger boot, and room for a cramped passenger or more luggage behind the seats. It was much more the high-speed roadster than the previous two-seater MGs had been, with its high top-gear ratio of 3.9:1.

From the car's introduction, the British press affected to find the MGB 'old-fashioned'. Announcing the new car in October 1962, *Motor Sport* remarked that the rumoured independent rear suspension had not materialized, and in its subsequent road-test observed that it remained a sports car in the best British, rather antiquated tradition.

The production engine was now good for an additional 800 rpm, peaking at 6,800 rpm, a figure which gave the useful maxima of 55 and 91 mph in second and third gears. The compression ratio was now 8.75:1, which made it necessary for the new 98 or 100 octane fuels to be used. Road-testers generally found the car provided an acceptable compromise between the need for sports-car firmness in suspension and the greater comfort now expected by the wider market at which the MGB

was aimed. The unitary structure brought a feeling of tautness, and the whole car felt immensely sturdy and rigid, helped by reassuringly predictable understeering handling characteristics.

The MGB engine underwent several important changes in the long years ahead, one of the most significant being from three to five bearings, as in the ADO 17, the front-wheel-drive 1800 saloon, in October 1964, when an oil cooler was also standardized. Overdrive had been made available the previous year, and these and other changes were intended to keep pace with competitors such as Triumph, who were progressively improving their offerings.

The Midget also received attention, and in March 1964 fairly drastic amendments were introduced. The quarter-elliptics had turned out to be unsatisfactory with the power the uprated 1,098 cc engine now gave, and in the G-AN3 model they were replaced with half-elliptic springs. It was at this point that the A-series engine was given a stiffer crankshaft with 2-inch diameter journals and a new exhaust manifold. There was a new curved windscreen and surround, and anti-burst door locks with interior release handles reflected the company's response to the first stirrings of safety legislators in overseas markets. In its Mark II form the Midget had wind-up windows — possibly a necessary refinement now that the car was close to being a 100-mph performer.

In 1965 the MGB range was broadened by the arrival of the GT, a three-door version of the basic roadster with an attractively proportioned superstructure. The origins of the design go back to early-1962, when Pininfarina built an Austin-Healey 3000 to the ideas of students from Ulm University, who had won an international design competition organized by a continental motoring yearbook. The car attracted a fair amount of attention at the London Motor Show that year, *Motor Sport* observing: 'At the moment there are no plans to put the car on the market, but with BMC one never knows'. EX 227 was the code number for Abingdon's GT project, and when Pininfarina was called in to advise on the styling in 1964, the prize-winning design was taken off the shelf and turned into production form very quickly, Enever being very much its midwife.

The MGB GT appeared at the 1965 London Motor Show and was scheduled to appear on the US market, for which it was mainly intended, in the spring of 1966. A road-test report appeared in *Road & Track* that May, and the testers showed a better awareness of the coupe's objectives than most UK writers achieved. They found it one of the quieter-running small sports-touring cars they had tested, although they said that overdrive would be valuable to avoid a disturbing resonance at 4,000 rpm (exactly 70 mph). Although the ride was still firm, the car's performance was not very wild, so there was less need than on some cars for a sophisticated suspension linkage. They found the rigidity of the coupe Gibraltar-like, but declared the disc-drum brakes susceptible to fade after repeated stops from 60 mph. Outright criticism of the non-synchromesh first gear and minor controls was expressed, but they would have liked to see the headlamp flasher arrangement universally adopted. The coupe was 224 lb heavier than the MGB roadster previously tested and had 4 bhp more, but it took only 1.1 seconds longer to 60 mph (13.6 against 12.5 seconds) and 19.6 seconds to the standing-quarter-mile against the roadster's 18.5 seconds.

It had a pleasant personality, it was fun and, yes, it was put together and finished properly. 'It could be more modern, but it could be less, too — long live the King', was how they ended their survey.

In 1967 the MGB Mark II appeared at Earls Court with an all-synchromesh wide-centre gearbox and with an automatic transmission available to choice, but the big news that year was the introduction of the six-cylinder MGC, regarded by many as the Austin-Healey 3000 replacement, but in truth more the product of Abingdon's desire to keep the basic structure of the MGB competitive. The MGC was not a very successful car in the marketplace. The problems that beset it reflected the doubts and uncertainties that surrounded BMC in the last 18 months before the series of mergers and negotiations that led at last to the announcement of a new giant motor corporation to be established through the amalgamation of the Leyland concern, which included Triumph sports cars, and British Motor Holdings, which included the former BMC marques and Jaguar.

Already, research into safety design and emission and pollution control was beginning to absorb an undue amount of the limited resources available to Abingdon. The ADO 52 project was tried-out with engines as diverse as the 2½-litre and 4½-litre Daimler V-8 units (in widened-body form), and the Coventry Climax V-8 of Grand Prix renown, as well as an ultra-short variant of the B-series with six cylinders. It appears that the Rover V-8 was not considered at the time because production capacity was insufficient for Rover's own needs. A new large-car project was under consideration at Longbridge, and the six-cylinder unit that at last appeared for Enever and his team to install in the MGC was intended for that. It was 210 lb heavier than the B-series unit and taller than anticipated, but although it was heavy it was very strong and it could have provided the power that was needed had development work continued. To install this awkward engine it was necessary to adopt torsion-bar front suspension, since the MGB cross-member was the wrong shape and had to be changed and the loads on the structure had to be sustained at a different part of the body.

The gearbox was modified and the rear axle, similar to that on Jaguars, had a 3:1 ratio in the manual form (later reduced to 3.3:1 to improve acceleration). There were bigger wheels and the MGC tipped the scales at 23 cwt. Despite the increase in engine weight, the actual weight distribution was disturbed only marginally, with just over 2 per cent increase on the front wheels. But the centre of gravity of the car was raised by the larger wheels and the (comparatively skinny) 165 x 15 tyres. When it was launched to the press at Silverstone the car's inherent problems in handling due to the much greater polar moment of inertia (compared with the MGB) resulting from the location of the mass of the engine were not fully understood and a uniformly bad reception was the result. In *Car,* Setright said it was, '. . . betrayed by front-end waywardness when it is not being tricked by rear-axle tramp'. In *Autosport,* Bolster said, 'by really flinging the car into the sharper corners, with full power on, the resultant rear-end breakaway is sudden, whilst the rear axle indulges in some unexpected capers, which discourages the driver from repeating the manoeuvre'. But its straight-line running was arrow-like.

The C was never able to overcome this early disparagement, and production ceased after nearly 9,000 had been built. Yet possibly it is the modern MG which more than any other has gathered around itself a group of defenders. Certainly in the lightweight, alloy-panelled version with light-alloy engine it was a dashing contender in long-distance events such as the Sebring 12-hours race, and had the new British Leyland's corporate leanings been towards Abingdon rather than to the determined Triumph protagonists led by Webster, a most remarkable high-speed tourer could have evolved. Successful sports cars have been known to emerge from an even more inauspicious beginning than that of the MGC.

By way of contrast, the Midget was steadily improved season by season. The Mark III of 1966 had a new folding hood frame, large rear-window panel and a larger cockpit opening to accommodate the folded hood, but more important it had one of the 1,275-cc engines, a production version of the Cooper S engine which had been so successful in all kinds of competition. In the Midget it had a 10-stud head and smaller ports, giving 64 bhp on a 8.7:1 compression ratio; power later went up to 70 bhp, but as legal requirements began to multiply, the car's sturdy powerplant began to lose ground. *Autocar's* 1971 road-test recorded a mean maximum of 94 mph with a standing-start quarter-mile time of 19.6 seconds and overall fuel consumption of 29.6 mpg. *Autocar* regarded the state of tune as 'inexplicably mild' and would have liked to have seen the car developed considerably, 'without losing its worthy character of sports-car primer for the not-so-well-off younger driver'.

CHAPTER EIGHT
The Grandest Tourer?

As the 1970s began there were three cars in the MG range: the 1300 saloon, offered by now with two doors only, the Midget and the MGB in roadster and GT guise. Unmourned, the Magnette had slipped into oblivion after reaching Mark IV status.

Apart from the basic engineering and equipment improvements that the engineers tried to bring in as they could, they were increasingly involved in trying to meet international safety regulations, particularly those introduced in the USA after the 1966 Safety Act of President Johnson. Each year it became harder: safety requirements included energy-absorbing steering columns, padded facia panels, safety belt and belt anchorage points to minimum standards and barrier-impact tests. As a result the period was not one of rapid change in automotive technology, and instead existing practice was refined and improved. Cars such as the MGB and the Midget could be progressively improved more readily than replaced by a company that was finding it increasingly difficult to finance new models and was in any case uncertain about its direction.

For Abingdon the biggest consolation of this period must have been that independent suspension all round was no longer considered as essential for the well-dressed sports car as it had been in previous years. A new generation of high-performance small saloons from Ford's competition department, joined later by the Triumph Dolomite, followed continental models like the Fiat 124 coupe in demonstrating that a fairly light rear axle carefully controlled by radius-arms could be non-independent and still give long suspension travel and taut handling. In truth, the MGB's suspension was much less sophisticated, but it was still very good, even if the ride on occasion was not up to the standard of later competitors.

Meanwhile, for the Midget, too, there was competition in the early-1970s. To a new generation of young enthusiasts brought up to expect to see competition drivers lying flat on their backs and manipulating miniature steering wheels, little coupes such as the Ginetta G15 were a new ideal; rear-engined overhead-camshaft performance was combined with fuel economy and superb handling, and the driver could lie back in the cockpit enjoying finger-tip steering and the flair of the styling. Of the big manufacturers, Fiat, with the mid-engined, Bertone-styled X1/9, seemed to have the future trend in small sports cars well weighed-up.

But even for journalists with those leanings, re-acquaintance with the Midget could bring re-appraisal. *Motor Sport* said: 'The performance is very much better than I had remembered. The A-series engine in 1275 form may be old-fashioned, but it still does the job extremely well, if a little harshly. The gearbox proved an absolute delight to use, being extremely quick apart from the lack of synchromesh in first, while the brakes stop the car well.' The old Midget, upright seating position and all, still had some life left in it.

If the fancy took an owner, the Midget could be handed over the the British Leyland Special Tuning people down at Abingdon. A full-race 11-stud head on Mini-Cooper S-type lines could be fitted for a quite modest charge in 1970, and there could be new pistons to bring the compression ratio up to 11.5:1, at which point a not too costly nitrided crankshaft would no doubt have been recommended. As engine speed could now be up to 7,800 rpm, a balanced engine was needed, and of course the legendary 648 camshaft would have gone in, matched by twin 1½-inch choke carburettors. Power would have been raised to 97 bhp at maximum rpm, and at that figure the Midget would have had a better power-to-weight ratio than the standard Lotus Super Seven.

While the Midget held its own, Abingdon looked once again for a way to update the MGB, which by 1973 had achieved the status of a classic in its own right. Just as the Morgan typified a particular period in sports car design, yet could readily be updated, so the MGB concept — so totally of the early-1960s — was to prove capable of development in the 1970s without losing its unique character.

It was strong, well-developed, and when the B-series engine was subjected to the expert attention of a specialist tuner, it could take on a new, fierce character. Just what could be done is illustrated by Bill Nicholson's racing MGB, which has competed for many seasons and is now probably the most consistently successful sports car ever built. In the late-1960s this car, with a cylinder-head modified to take maximum rpm up to 7,000, gave around 140 bhp from its three-bearing engine of 1,788 cc. Lightened to 17½ cwt and with a factory hardtop fitted, its 0-100 mph time was 19.9 seconds and on the short straights of Silverstone circuit 122 mph was registered during a test drive by *Motor Sport*. The handling was in keeping with such performance, and the Nicholson racing shop offered tuning in stages.

For a still quite modest outlay a keen driver could buy a modified and gas-flowed cylinder-head with an improved exhaust manifold, matched by larger SUs, and attention to the suspension, which included lower springs and a strong anti-roll bar at the front. Power was estimated to be up to 107 bhp and the 0-60 mph time was 11 seconds, matched by a top speed as high as 117 mph. Impressive though all this was, the reliability of engines subjected to such attention would not necessarily be as high and consistent as the factory would need if it was to give the kind of warranty that modern legislation and practice demands.

Another approach was needed, and a pointer was given by Ken Costello, from Kent, a one-time Mini driver who realized that the old saying 'there's no substitute for litres' held good for MGBs, too. He started installing the lightweight aluminium Rover V-8 3½-litre engine in MGBs for his customers. Since the Rover was both very light and very compact for its swept volume, it fitted in very neatly, and when suitable changes were made to the running gear, the Costello V-8 MGB became an effortless high-speed tourer, with none of the handling problems that had so beset the old MGC.

It could only be a matter of time before an Abingdon V-8 appeared and sure enough, in August 1973, Abingdon's grandest tourer was announced.

By 1972 British Leyland had become the major research establishment for the nation's vehicle safety programmes. Under government sponsorship, some important work was to be carried out and the company's safety engineers were soon in a position to make significant contributions. At a period when the American solution was to produce a kind of armoured passenger car of hideous appearance and abysmal roadholding, Abingdon took an MGB and built SSV 1 on the principle that secondary safety such as seat belts and collapsible steering columns were all very well, but if the car was not fundamentally sound in all areas of roadholding, handling and braking, the end product was likely to be disappointing. Their first solution was shown at an important road safety symposium held in Washington DC in spring 1972, where it received a favourable reception.

The SSV 1 was intended at least in part to be a publicity exercise, and in consequence it was not surprising to see in the vehicle a number of features which have sunk without making any great impact, but one of the most unexpected disappearances is that of the sophisticated electronic four-wheel brake anti-locking system by Automotive Products and Lucas/Girling. More important, from the standpoint of the sports-car designer, was a paper presented by BL's chief safety engineer, who began from the position: '. . . it is evident that avoidance of accidents is no less a priority than occupant protection and that the handling and stability of vehicles is a subject of great importance'.

From this promising beginning he went on to look at the various aspects of handling and stability, including steady-state response (following a curved path), transient-state response (changing rapidly from one road lane to another), time lag between the driver's input and his car's response, and practical handling tests, which involved investigations into yaw.

His observations provided valuable information, highlighting the important effects on yaw inertia and hence handling responses, both of total weight — the greater the weight the greater the yaw inertia and the more the response — and of the exact location of the major masses in relation to the vehicle's centre of gravity. Other findings concerned the need for tyres with high lateral stiffness for best response. A long wheelbase gives good response, too, at the expense of a poor turning circle. It was all highly relevant to the new large-engined MGB variant.

When, in the early-1960s, the Rover company realized they simply had to have a powerful new engine to take their very successful 2000 and 3-Litre range into the 1970s, they were in considerable difficulty. To raise the enormous capital sums needed for their new factories they had used up all their reserves and were now caught up in the stop-go policies imposed by successive Governments acting on uninformed advice proffered by civil servants. It was a situation that brought many companies to disaster, and Rover suffered severely from these constraints, so it must have been with a great sense of relief that the board heard that Managing Director Martin-Hurst had literally stumbled across a suitable engine during a visit to the USA.

Coincidentally, the engine and the body structure of what was to become the MGB V8 were both first shown to the public in 1965. In the spring Rover showed to a few selected journalists a 3-Litre saloon with their new 3½-litre light-alloy engine installed; the MGB was unveiled at that year's London Motor Show. The V-8 engine was originally created by General Motors for a new compact Buick, but when the expected market for that size of car faded it was discarded, leaving it free for Rover to take up under licence. It was light and compact, but it needed development to meet European requirements. Despite a robust crankshaft and the excellent breathing possibilities inherent in its layout, engine speeds above 4,800 rpm showed up weaknesses in the pistons and valve gear.

Rover's manufacturing technology was not adapted to the methods used by the engine's originators, involving casting with liners in situ, but instead new methods of thin-wall aluminium casting were evolved for it. The short-stroke, big-bore engine had five crankshaft bearings and the inclined overhead valves were actuated by hydraulic lifters and rockers from the central camshaft. The original units developed 150 bhp gross at 4,400 rpm and by the middle of 1967 Rover had installed twin carburettors, reduced the compression ratio slightly and achieved 160 bhp gross. By the time the Rover 3500 appeared, in 1968, power was up to 184 bhp gross at 5,200 rpm with outstanding reliability and very long life.

In the MG application, with an 8.25:1 compression ratio, maximum bhp was 137 DIN at 5,000 rpm; torque was 193 lb ft at 2,900 rpm. With both the head and the block of light-alloy the basic V-8 engine was some 40 lb lighter than the 1.8-litre 'four', but with the inevitable complexity and weight of the ancillary equipment now essential to meet noise, emission and safety regulations, the total weight rose to just over that of the 1.8-litre unit. Most of the extra weight went on to the front wheels, the ratio from front to rear being 49.4/50.6 per cent compared with the 47.8/52.2 split of the four-cylinder model. The SU HIF6 (horizontal integral float chamber) carburettors were designed to provide stable carburation under all conditions of hard cornering, acceleration and braking. They were installed at the rear of the engine on a specially designed manifold evolved by Abingdon to give dual benefits of greatly reduced temperature scatter from one cylinder to another, compared with the original penthouse manifold, while at the same time avoiding the need for a power bulge on the bonnet's smooth contours. Neat bimetallic valves were arranged to draw in warm air at first, from sleeves on the exhaust manifold, then to take in cooler air when the engine was warm.

Detail modifications to the all-synchromesh C-type gearbox (itself derived from the 'B') were necessary, and the gearbox casing was strengthened and redesigned to accept a larger clutch. As the torque was almost double, intermediate gear ratios were raised to match the different output curve and to reduce the torque load in the box, which was close to its limit, even with the basic engine. The axle ratio was 3.07:1 against the 3.9:1 of the four-cylinder version and came down to 2.5:1 on overdrive fourth — long legs indeed. There was a minor modification to the front cross-member and the rear bulkhead, and the inner wheelarches were also changed. The rear springs were substantially stiffened to control the increased torque, and the front anti-roll bar was repositioned, while the steering rack went forward one inch. To replace the four-inch instruments previously fitted there were new 80-mm speedometer and tachometer displays, a change brought about by the need to provide space for the collapsible steering column on right-hand-drive versions.

The MGB GT V8 came out at a difficult time for British Leyland. The company was floundering in a sea of criticism both of its products and of its own internal problems, and was to run headlong into the consequences of the prolonged miners' strike, which were complicated by the long-term effects of the Arab oil embargo and the abrupt upgrading of their oil prices.

This new MG was aimed at a very clearly defined section of the market. Throughout Europe there was a growing demand for the so-called two-plus-two GT car, closed, fast, comfortable and capable of taking two occupants and all their luggage long distances at high speeds with a minimum of fuss or fatigue. The V8 was priced a resounding £500 more than the similarly equipped four-cylinder model, but at £2,293 it was in competition with the Reliant Scimitar GTE (£2,430), the Datsun 240Z (£2,535), the Lotus Elan Plus 2 S130 (£2,789) and the Triumph Stag (£2,533). The only real competitor which underpriced the V8 was the Ford Capri 3000 GXL at £1,824.

It was not in any way intended to be an out-and-out sports car — with a compression ratio similar to that of the Range Rover it was not likely to be that — but it did compare very well with others in its price class. As *Motor* observed, only the Morgan Plus 8 and the Lotus Elan Sprint were faster to 60 mph and only the lighter-bodied Morgan was anywhere near on top-gear performance. Most of the testers approved of the handling, the brakes were well able to cope, and the straight-line running was uniformly said to be good, although — possibly as a result of the straight-running stability — some felt that the steering was on the heavy side. *Autocar's* test summed it up: 'The combination of the timeless lines of the Pininfarina-influenced MGB GT and the smoothness of the lightweight 3,582-cc Rover V8 engine ought, on paper anyway, to make for an excellent high-performance sporting coupe.' If in the end the product fell short in any way it was in 'unfortunate perpetuation of the dated features of the MGB. Such shortcomings as excessive wind noise, a harsh ride and heavy steering may be forgiven in an out-and-out sports car, but they have no place in a car costing over £2,000'.

Still, the remarkable smoothness and refinement of the engine, they admitted, went most of the way to making up for the less likable facets of the car. It was an economical combination, recording 23 mpg overall on road-test, and at 28.5 mph per 1,000 rpm in overdrive it was remarkably long-legged.

The MGB GT V8 — it was never offered in roadster form for reasons to do with structural stiffness — was right in all the areas where the MGC was deficient, for its creators were now much more aware of the importance of weight distribution in determining yaw inertia and hence basic handling characteristics. In terms of its engineering, then, the MGB V8 was successful. It had all the power the rugged body needed; handling, stability and braking were well in keeping; its ability to cover great distances in an effortless manner was conceded by the toughest critics; but it gradually faded away and at the end, just before production ceased after less than 2,600

had been made, it was in effect only being turned out to special order. These days some manufacturers build greater numbers of their 'limited edition' models.

What went wrong? In the first place it was never considered feasible to sell the car in the USA, which must have been identified as potentially the GT V8's major market outlet from the beginning. 'The cost of Type Approval would presumably be prohibitive,' was the explanation offered by the usually sympathetic *Autocar,* and indeed neither the Range Rover nor the Rover V-8 saloons had been submitted to the strict American 'anti-smog' legislators at that time. But there was also the question of Rover's limited V-8 production capacity at its Acocks Green plant, where the production managers had to balance the MG company's need against their own pressing necessity to boost output of the immensely successful Range Rover. As the two-year gestation period of the essentially simple engine change suggested, it was availability rather than suitability which limited the MGB V8's success.

Finally cut-off by circumstances from its major market, the car had to rely on European sales, and here the after-effects of the Arab's oil embargo, with petrol prices sky-high in countries such as France and Germany, with rationing and restrictions on the recreational use of automobiles in others such as Holland, meant that the attention of potential buyers came to be focussed on much smaller-engined competitors. Perhaps, if the stylists had thought to make the car more readily distinguishable from its much cheaper sisters, the status-conscious Europeans might have been more strongly attracted, but as it was, Abingdon's highest-performance production model — the K3 and Q-type notwithstanding — quietly dropped out of the buyers' guides in 1976.

'With the need for model rationalization,' said the company before the Motor Show in London that autumn, 'and increased MGB production for the USA market, the low-volume MGB GT V8 model has been discontinued, to concentrate resources on the soft-top MGB and hatchback MGB GT models.'

The next paragraph of this release made interesting reading, for the MG Midget 1500 soft-top would continue in unchanged form in 1977. In fact the 1500 engine had crept quietly into the Midget in October 1974, curiously enough a couple of months before its appearance in the Triumph Spitfire, though the latter model already had the same unit in 1300 form. This engine, with 73.7 ×

87.5 mm bore and stroke, was of 1,493 cc, and in the twin-carburettor Midget version it gave 71 bhp. It derived from a four-cylinder 803-cc unit announced in 1953 which was used to power the plump little Standard Ten. It seems very likely that the new engine had been designed after its builders had digested what Austin's A-series had to offer, and the biggest point of difference was that much more 'stretch' was built into it. Evolution of this unit in the successful Spitfire — 200,000 sold in nearly 11 years to August 1973 — to combat increasing car weight and restricted breathing due to emission control and safety equipment, paralleled that of the Midget's A-series unit, with an intermediate 1,147-cc version giving 63 bhp.

By 1976 the Spitfire and the Midget were brisk competitors of each other, the Midget having most of the advantages on paper, with a 101 mph top speed (100 mph for the Spitfire), and acceleration time from 0 to 60 mph of 12.3 seconds (13.2 seconds for the Spitfire). It was also slightly cheaper than the Spitfire, but at 27.9 mpg the fuel economy was worse than the 29.2 mpg of the Triumph. The two cars were very different in character, with the Spitfire offering an easier ride, more space in the cockpit and a tiny turning circle, but with the Midget ahead in nimbleness and general handling, appealing much more as the enthusiast's car.

The MGB, too, had a major competitor with the arrival of the TR7 from Triumph in May 1976. Although with an overhead-camshaft four-cylinder engine and MacPherson-strut suspension at the front-end, matched by coil-spring, radius-arm and live-axle rear suspension, it appeared a simple design, the TR7 was of the new generation of sports models offering both taut handling and a superb ride. Equipped with a 2-litre version of the Dolomite slant-four engine, on test it gave a 109 mph top speed and a 0 to 60 mph time of 9.1 seconds. It was only just cheaper than the MGB GT.

The MGB did not show to advantage in paper comparisons with the TR7; weighing more and with a smaller engine it could hardly be expected to. Even worse, during 1975 the heavy bumpers adopted to meet Federal regulations concerning 5-mph impacts — the Americans required that in such impacts no safety-related systems such as brakes or steering would be damaged — had made it necessary to raise the ride height of the car by 1½ inches to the detriment of the handling. In 1976 the MGB's top speed was 105 mph and 0 to 60 mph occupied 12.1 seconds, and its overall fuel consumption was 26.1 mpg against the 28 mpg of the Triumph. But the styling of the TR7 was controversial, and misunderstandings about the scope of future American regulations had led to the omission of a soft-top version, while the open MGB roadster still soldiered on. Even so, there was much conjecture at this period about the MG's future. It was believed that a body of opinion was in favour of phasing-out the MG name in favour of Triumph under British Leyland's corporate plans. A succession of financial crises involving the departure of one chief executive after another, plus the wide-ranging Ryder Report — which was rapidly shelved when it was decided to adopt another, less fully integrated approach to managing the many different plants in the company — did little to create confidence in the minds of MG enthusiasts all over the world.

As it happened, these gloomy thoughts were premature. By 1977 Abingdon had been able to repair much of the damage done to the car's qualities by all the mandatory equipment it now wore on engine and body structure. But they were not able to do much about the weight problem, for by this time the GT's kerbside weight was up to 21.8 cwt, to the detriment of its acceleration, which by now took 14 seconds from 0 to 60 mph. Many everyday saloons could outrun the car, but they could not match the 16-year-old design in its most pleasing and enjoyable handling. Said *Autocar* in its road test: 'The B has never been the sort of sports car to set standards of roadholding . . . Rather the pleasure of driving it has come from the taut and predictable reactions. An initial modest understeer gives way as cornering speeds build up, to readily controllable oversteer. Ultimate levels of roadholding are not high, but the car's controllability makes it fun to drive'. That passage, indeed, says as much about the changing face of motoring journalism as it does about the car.

The engineers had adopted conventional methods of improving the suspension. No change could be made to the ride height, but the open roadster received an anti-roll bar on its front suspension for the first time, while that of the GT was made thicker. At the rear, an anti-roll bar was fitted for the first time, the 'Police' rear springs fitted to the GT on its introduction in 1965 no longer being able to cope with the forces upon them. Apart from the changes to improve handling, the opportunity was taken to meet most of the criticisms levelled at the car's instrumentation and equipment over the years, since it had changed little for over a decade.

The instruments were re-arranged, and the facia itself was revised to give a more logical and accessible layout for the controls and switches. The heater controls were improved and details such as the lock for the facia cubby hole were improved at last. The most striking change was to brightly striped fabric for the seats, which were unchanged in structure.

To reduce steering effort despite the greater weight, the steering ratio was increased from three to three-and-a-half turns lock-to-lock, although the wheel diameter was reduced to 15 inches, which tended to minimize the benefits brought by the new ratio.

Although advertising in the USA for MG had had its share of inanities — a 1975 Golden Anniversary advertisement talked about Nuvolari at Le Mans (he was, but never in an MG) — they sometimes produced seductive copy which went close to the heart of the MGB's appeal: '. . . still most at home on twisting ribbons of almost forgotten scenic routes where cars go to be driven, not scorched off the line in a brute display of acceleration'.

Or again: 'With direct rack-and-pinion steering, 10.5-inch front disc brakes, race-seasoned suspension, four-speed close-ratio gearbox and a high-performance, overhead-valve engine — all the world is road. Even in the fiercely competitive world of racing, MGB excels in its class. It's the reigning SCCA National Champion in E Production.' That was in the early-1970s, but it was to be the same in the years ahead, for in 1977 an MGB won the SCCA National Championship in Class E again, driven by Terry Visger and prepared by Huffaker Engineering.

Nobody sneered at MG's pretensions to be a sports car in the USA. The image was not the one that the British enthusiast had, of a tall GT coupe perched on lean wheels and tyres. The picture in the USA was of a modern, well-sorted MGB sports-racer, low, wide, fully-flared in the bodyshell to take broad-shouldered racing tyres. It was a car which won season after season in the long and demanding SCCA Championship series and it was fully expected to keep on winning.

To bring it to this level a considerable amount of development was permitted by the regulations. The Huffaker Engineering cars gave at least 156 bhp, and although the engine was considered to be on the heavy side, this characteristic did at least hold out a prospect of reliability, a hope often fully rewarded, for in the 1974 season Visger competed in 19 E-Production races, winning 17 of

them in a car that had been campaigned for eight seasons. Standard tuning practice was followed, with attention to breathing, valve timing and the reduction of the weight of rotating and reciprocating parts. An MGB Competition Manual was written by Huffaker and produced by British Leyland Motors of USA. It contained the practical information that amateur drivers needed, with emphasis on meticulous attention to detail and perfect cleanliness.

The racing rear axle was located by radius-arms and a Panhard rod, while the front-end had 1½ degrees negative camber and heavier coil springs. Altogether the ride height was reduced by 1½ inches in pre-Federal-height days, which means that in post-Federal specification conditions the racing SCCA MGB was three inches lower than in road-going form. Wider wheels giving a two-inch increase in track were permitted, and the brakes were modified to give an adjustable front-rear ratio with twin master-cylinders.

In Britain, too, the MGB went racing; the incredible car of Bill Nicholson had covered an estimated 38,250 racing miles in his hands in 10 years between 1963 and 1973, but racing at club level the publicity impact was not so great. In important international long-distance events the racing B and C versions put up remarkable performances until the beginning of the 1970s, and these efforts with Abingdon-prepared examples of close to standard machines, particularly at Sebring, against a new generation of much more aerodynamically sophisticated sports-racers, will surely be seen in the future as a fascinating passage in the long story of the thoroughbreds from Abingdon.

CHAPTER NINE

'MG Enthusiast of the Year'

When it was announced that there had been a change of policy favouring individual makes in British Leyland, it was not very long before the octagon symbol began to reappear throughout the Abingdon plant. Individual marques were to be promoted, and the always enthusiastic people at the MG's home knew what was needed. Their open day in September 1977 was an enormous success, and the demand for tickets for employees and their families was so great it could not be satisfied. For

MG owners from all over the world it was a place of pilgrimage; even the most regular visitors to the place felt a slight stir of pride in a factory that contributed so much to motoring history.

Near the main road, just by the double gates where the great transporters brought in the bodyshells, there was the little patch of lawn where Magic Midget once stood, with Eyston and little Denly proudly facing the camera. Walk down Cemetery Road to the old office block where Kimber sat and where the plant director still held court with a great Gordon Crosby painting over the fireplace in the wooden-panelled office, and you passed the stone wall where the C-type Midgets waited before they left for Brooklands and the Double Twelve in 1931. There was the iron frame of the factory weighbridge still set flush in the tarmac before you got to the modern swinging gate. Just inside was the lean-to shed where the cars were put through their final test and washed before their owners came to collect them.

MGs were built in a particular way, and the workers took an interest in their products. When local brewers Morrell ran a poll to choose a name for a new pub in a nearby Abingdon suburb, Magic Midget was the winning name, but most suggestions had an MG theme. Men tended to stay at the factory, and in 1975 it was estimated that the individual length of service averaged between 10 and 20 years.

Production rates were high — nobody pretended the MG was anything but a mass-production sports car — but one plant director observed, 'there's an art in assembly and most of our production workers have got the art'. To give the satisfaction that workers can get from their eight-hour daily stint, work-cycle times were long, with between nine and 15 minutes favoured, which meant that a man had the satisfaction of completing a job rather than merely doing a part of it.

In the tightly regulated world that a modern sports car inhabits, testing and inspection undreamt of by yesterday's builders is mandatory. Sophisticated new test cells and laboratories were built, but few were to do with improving the basic car. Rather the need was to spend much time, money and effort on crash-testing, and on emission and pollution control. Experiments had to continue to keep abreast of continually changing international legislation.

As it came off the production line, each MG was checked-out on a roller-tester, which determined electronically exactly how much power the engine gave and the state of adjustment of the brakes and steering. Eight per cent of the production was also road-tested. It was a far cry from the 'run down the Marcham road' of prewar days and the blast on the Comparator, which as Cousins said, 'really only worked properly at full throttle'.

In 1978, Abingdon covered some 41.7 acres, with buildings accounting for nine acres. It employed 1,200 people with six unions to represent them. Every year it used 5,000,000 gallons of water, 85,000 therms of gas, 450,000 gallons of fuel oil and 3,000,000 kilowatt-hours of electricity.

Well over 1,000,000 MGs had been built at Abingdon, and on a good week production could rise to 1,400 cars, of which 80 per cent were exported; Leonard Lord would have been delighted, especially as the line was still not fully mechanized. It also housed the tuning shops from which the works TR7 issued to battle its way through rally championship events, as well as the BL Advanced Driving School.

In the autumn of 1978 MG was moved from Austin-Morris to Jaguar-Rover-Triumph within the BL Cars Limited structure. At the time it seemed a fairly logical move. Although the mechanical parts of the MG models had no connection at all with any other JRT car, it was the JRT branch which had experience of selling in the North American market, where most MG cars were sold. but the doubts remained. Abingdon had begun to look very exposed. As disaster followed disaster within BL Cars and the company's losses mounted, observers wondered whether there could be a place for the MG name. The B model was now sadly outmoded, the Midget surely at the end of its life.

Philip Turner of *Motor* asked those very questions of the JRT managers and the answer he got was published in May 1979.

'MG? We'd be crazy to ditch it. Next to Jaguar it's the most valuable name JRT possess.' That, said Turner, was the united and very firm view of the Jaguar Rover Triumph management, and the same went for Abingdon, a good plant with a good workforce and good industrial relations which it would be 'stupid to abandon'.

Indeed, in the early months of 1979, it still seemed that there was a long-term future for the MGB or a derivative. The Midget was to be phased-out in favour of the Triumph Spitfire, which outsold it in the USA, but it seemed likely that a 2-litre version of the new O-series engine, itself an overhead-camshaft second-generation edition of the ancient B-series unit, would be installed in an extensively facelifted MGB which would continue to appeal to the market that supposedly existed for a 'traditional' sports car lying somewhere between the 1935-style Morgan and more modern designs such as the Datsun, Fiat and TR7.

In May, *Motor* published a comparative test in which the MGB and the Midget were ranged alongside the Spitfire and two formidable continental high-performance saloons, the Alfasud 1.5ti and the Renault R5 Gordini. Not surprisingly, given the 17 years or so between the designs, the Alfasud and the Renault showed well, particularly in terms of lively performance and value for money, although the testers thought the MGs had their own appeal as open cars, 'when the sun was out'.

By August 1979 500,000 MGBs had been sold and to outsiders demand still seemed healthy in the USA. On the other hand, output of the Midget was being reduced to 150 a week in anticipation of phasing it out later in the year. To take up the slack, MGB production was to be boosted to 750 a week, the bodyshells were to be trimmed at Abingdon instead of Cowley as before, and the Vanden Plas 1500 was being transferred from the North London factory where they had previously been finished. Production of these fat little saloons, based on the front-wheel-drive Austin Allegro, was set at 20 a week.

Abingdon town prepared to celebrate the Golden Jubilee of the MG factory in early-September 1979. It all began on a Saturday evening with a fireworks gala. During the week-long festivities there was an exhibition of MG history, raft races on the Thames, a barbecue and a grand procession of MG cars through the town to the MG sports club playing field. An MGB roadster was lifted into the air by a hot air balloon. It was, everybody agreed, a thoroughly enjoyable occasion.

But even before the celebrations began clouds were gathering over the marque. You had to be alert to notice them. On August 31 a perceptive *Financial Times* journalist mused: '. . . the fate of the Midget itself cannot but raise questions about what long-term future is envisaged for the anachronistic Abingdon operation under the policy umbrella of its Jaguar Rover Triumph parent . . . Abingdon concedes that a burst of British inflation coupled with the strength of the pound could easily turn the B round from being the subject of an occasional US waiting list to unsold stocks . . .' Prophetic words indeed.

With seeming unconcern for the effect that their timing would have, BL Cars chose September 10 to announce that Abingdon production of the MG was to cease. The news broke, as the *Daily*

Telegraph reflected, while staff were still clearing up after the company's Golden Jubilee celebrations. No detailed reasons were given for the closure decision at this stage and no production figures were available. It was known that the four MGB lines were shut because of a lack of components, principally axles. The only work in hand was on Midgets.

Stung by what they clearly saw as unfair criticism of their insensitivity, BL Cars hastened to justify their decision to close Abingdon and on September 26 claimed they were suffering a loss of £900 on every MGB sold in the USA. The steep fall in the value of the dollar against sterling was blamed and by the end of 1979 BL let it be known that they had lost £20 million in 12 months on Abingdon and its products. Meanwhile, an emotional 'Save MG' campaign was gathering momentum and the MG motor clubs organized parades and petitions to BL Cars.

At the height of all the excitement a new figure arrived on the scene. A normally stoic *Sunday Times* reporter thought that Alan Curtis sounded: 'very like one of Buchan's gentlemanly middle-aged heroes, keen on loyalty and fair play and a born leader of men'. With the American Peter Sprague, Curtis had taken over the loss-making Aston Martin concern and was now co-chairman. The company had cost them £1 million and during 1979 it was to return its first profits for many seasons on a production of seven or eight V-8 Aston Martins a week.

Curtis believed that his company's expertise would perfectly complement the world-renowned pedigree of MG. The marriage between the two makes had a certain logic. Aston Martin was in an exposed position with its minute production of costly automobiles and a higher-production-rate and cheaper second string looked like a good idea. The skills were there, for had not Aston just taken on the experienced John Symonds from BL's Cowley plant, where he had been production chief?

During a phone call on October 14 to his co-chairman Sprague in the USA, Curtis was told: 'Go out and get it'. The next day he set up a preliminary meeting in Oxford, and on October 16 brought together in the Grosvenor House Hotel in London the elements of a consortium to make a takeover bid for MG. At this time those involved included David Wickins of British Car Auctions, the Norwest Construction Group and Peter Cadbury (then chairman of Westward Television). It was hoped to raise up to £30 million between them. On the other side of Mayfair on the same day, a disgruntled group of BL's USA car distributors was closeted with Sir Michael Edwardes of BL to plead for a stay of execution for MG.

On October 17, Abingdon Member of Parliament Tom Benyon formed a group of Conservative Party MPs to press for reconsideration of the closure decision. A couple of days later BL Cars made it known to selected pressmen that neither the Abingdon plant nor the MG trademark were for sale. 'There is', said *The Guardian* thoughtfully, 'a certain naivety about the bid by Mr Curtis . . . and Mr David Wickins of the British Car Auctions Group. Whatever might be the image of MG, the marque has always relied heavily on components produced within the group. Any takeover is bound to run into problems.'

The largest single problem was that 85 per cent of the MGB came from 12 other factories in the group and 80 per cent of that was now unique to the car. Meanwhile, the winding-down programme went on. The last large order for Midgets, from Japan, was put in hand.

For the next six months or so the negotiations were to take many turns, but the underlying fact was always that Aston Martin really wanted to take over the plant, the car and the name, and that was precisely what BL was unwilling to give up. Prudence dictated that the TR7 ought to be protected. It really had not been too successful in the USA, its main market, and from BL's point of view a revitalized MGB would be an unwelcome competitor. By the end of October 1979 Curtis was beginning to see that a licensing deal was the one most likely to emerge. 'It would be a move in the right direction,' he told reporters. 'But I think that the jobs of 1,100 people at Abingdon are going to be very important and that means the factory has got to come as well.'

There was still £30 million on the table. According to Wickins it was, 'more money available than we need to do the thing'. Talks between BL and its USA dealers were getting harder and the possibility of legal action being taken if the supply of MGs was cut off was being spoken about. BL reprieved the MG on November 6. 'They will be available until 1981,' said BL. 'As our assurances to the American dealers made clear, BL wants to retain the MG marque.'

On a Saturday in mid-November, Curtis made a flying visit to the Abingdon plant under what the *Oxford Times* called, 'a veil of secrecy'. According to that incredulous *Sunday Times* man, Curtis, wearing an old suit and a cloth cap, arrived incognito to mingle 'inconspicuously' with the workers. At this stage it was thought that a facelift adding about £1,000 to the cost of each car would be essential to sell the MGB under the Aston Martin banner, and stylist Bill Towns, who was responsible for the startling appearance of the Lagonda Bulldog, was commissioned to prepare preliminary designs through the winter.

The last MG Midget rolled off the Abingdon line on December 12 carrying a coffin and the message: 'Gone but not Forgotten'. BL did not invite the press to this occasion. On the same day the consortium announced that they would be making their offer in about three weeks. Talks had been, 'of a meaningful nature'. BL had agreed that it might be able to switch some of the operations planned to replace MG at Abingdon to another location so that, 'a specialized vehicle unit could remain there'.

Coincidentally, Morris Garages, which still existed as a motor dealer, lost its Austin-Morris franchise and closed its two Oxford depots in mid-December. Its profitable Renault business continued in High Wycombe some 30 miles away.

As the old year drew to a close no firm offer had been made to BL, who allowed thoughts about a new MG sports car to appear in *The Guardian*: 'It will probably not be built at Abingdon, but alongside the TR7 at the Rover plant at Solihull'. MG was transferred back to Austin-Morris from the by now very troubled Jaguar-Rover-Triumph operation.

In mid-January 1980 there was the first suggestion that not all was well with the consortium. Peter Cadbury announced that they were to seek to raise £12 million from City sources by the end of January. If not, they could get all the money and working capital they needed from the Japanese. They had earmarked £100,000 to get the MGB's B-series engine through the crucial new US emission tests it would soon be facing. It was thought that MG could be very profitable in three years, producing a 20 per cent return on capital.

'We have a new engine on the drawing board and this would take about two years to develop,' explained Cadbury. In the meantime they would rely on BL to continue to produce engines for them to ensure continuity of sales in the USA. A formal offer was to be made on January 17, 1980, but by January 26 none had been received. *Autocar* commented sadly: 'It does seem really that at around this time next year the very last MGB will be rolling down the line at Abingdon'.

It all began to be a political issue towards the end

of March. A confidential letter from the Department of Industry to Brian Horrocks of BL assured him that the Government would not be erecting barriers to 'commercially based' judgments on the future of MG. Robert Adley MP, a member of a 'Save MG' group in the Commons, said that Secretary of State for Industry Sir Keith Joseph, 'should see himself as an oil-can, not a spanner,' in the MG matter.

Speaking to *Now!* magazine at the end of March, Alan Curtis said he was now, 'fairly doubtful if any deal will finally emerge. There was a change in philosophy halfway through the negotiations. We believed that the best solution for everybody was emerging and then something caused a spanner to be thrown into the works'.

At last, on the final day of March 1980, a deal was announced. It had been agreed in principle that the consortium could make the MG under licence at Abingdon. It had not been easy. Sir Michael himself had suggested the formation of British Sports Cars Limited, a joint marketing company. For some reason this sensible suggestion did not go ahead. Some press sources blamed what they called Sir Keith's 'rigid dogmatism'. Alan Curtis said he failed to understand why BL withdrew a suggestion it made itself. The intention had been that BL and Aston would each hold 40 per cent of the company and outsiders the remaining 20 per cent.

Then the months slipped by. A worldwide recession became a deep slump in the UK. Demand for the MGB began to slip. Abingdon went on to a three-day week, reducing output to 600 cars or less a week. Rumours began to spread about the deal. Mr Curtis was said to be in Japan. The MG enthusiasts were still optimistic. At an MG Car Club rally at Donington Park circuit in June Alan Curtis was declared 'MG Enthusiast of the Year'. The only shadow he could see over MG's future was the approaching period of economic gloom, but they were some way down the road to detoxing the O-series engine to satisfy US legislation.

At the end of June BL were getting restive. They announced that they were losing £400,000 every week on Abingdon. Sales of MGs were down 75 per cent on the previous year. Tim Hearley of C. H. Industrials bought a £450,000 stake in Aston Martin Lagonda. Then, on July 1, 1980 the consortium told Pratt Thompson, chairman of BL Cars, that they could not come up with the necessary finance. Investors had withdrawn. One million was the most that could be found. On the same day Aston announced that it was sacking 100 of its 460 workers and putting the rest on short time. Aston Martin production was down to a no longer profitable four to five cars a week. BL announced that there were 16,000 MGs unsold in world markets, 13,000 of them in the USA. Abingdon was going to be closed in October 24, 1980 and press attention was turned towards BL's Broadside project, which it was surmised was a four-seater coupe version of the TR7 and would be built alongside Rovers at Solihull. It was, they thought, the most likely car to carry the MG octagon in the future. On October 24, when the MG factory at Abingdon was duly closed at last, it was announced that 10,000 MGs were still unsold and stockpiled in the USA.

Alan Curtis, interviewed by *Motor* magazine, said he intended to take a two-month break in Bergerac, in France, to compile a book about the rescue attempt. In their pre-Christmas edition, the *Sunday Times* dubbed Curtis, 'Tryer of the Year'. 'No-one,' they said, not unkindly, 'can accuse Curtis of being less than genuine in his efforts to rescue the famous sports-car company and its 950-strong workforce at Abingdon.

'So he failed.'

APPENDIX
Technical specifications
and production figures

Raworth-bodied 11.9 – produced 1923 to 1924
Bodywork: Open 2-str. Engine: 4-cyl, side-valve, 69.5 × 102mm, 1,548cc, CR 5:1, SU carburettor, 24-28 bhp. Transmission: 3-speed gearbox, sliding pinion; final drive 4.7:1. Chassis: Wheelbase 8ft 6in, track 4ft; suspension ½-elliptic front, ¾-elliptic rear with shackles; brakes 9in rear only; wheels bolt-on artillery.

14/28 Super Sports – produced 1924 to 1926
Bodywork: Open 2-str, open 4-str, closed coupe and saloon. Engine: 4-cyl, side-valve, 75 × 102mm, 1,802cc, CR 5:1, SU or Smith carburettor, 30 bhp. Transmission: 3-speed gearbox, sliding pinion; final drive 4.42:1. Chassis: Wheelbase 8ft 6in or 9ft, track 4ft; suspension ½-elliptic front, ¾-elliptic rear with shackles; brakes 12in (servo 1925-6); wheels bolt-on artillery with disc cover.

14/28 and 14/40 Mk IV – produced 1926 to 1929
Bodywork: Open 2-str, open 4-str, closed coupe and saloon.Engine: 4-cyl, side-valve, 75 × 102mm, 1,802cc, CR 5:1, Solex carburettor, 35bhp @ 4,000 rpm. Transmission: 3-speed gearbox, sliding pinion; final drive 4.42:1. Chassis: Wheelbase 8ft 10½in, track 4ft; suspension ½-elliptic front and rear with shackles; brakes 12in (servo 1926-7); wheels bolt-on wire, tyres 4.95 × 19. First chassis number 2251.

18/80 Six Mk I and Mk II – produced 1928 to 1931
Bodywork: Open 2-str, open 4-str, closed coupe and saloon. Engine: 6-cyl, overhead-camshaft, chain-driven, 69 × 110mm, 2,468cc, CR 5.8:1, 2 SU carburettors, 60 bhp @ 3,200 rpm. Transmission: 3-speed (Mk I) or 4-speed (Mk II) gearbox, sliding pinion and remote control; final drive 4.25:1 (Mk I) or 4.27:1 (Mk II). Chassis: Wheelbase 9ft 6in, track 4ft (Mk I) or 4ft 4in (Mk II); suspension ½-elliptic front and rear with shackles; brakes 12in (Mk I) or 14in (Mk II), some cars with servo; wheels bolt-on (early models) or centre-lock wire, tyres 5.00 × 19. First chassis number 6750.

18/80 Six Mk III – produced 1930
Bodywork: Open 4-str. Engine: As Mk II except CR 6.9:1, 90-100 bhp according to tune. Transmission: As Mk II. Chassis: As Mk II. First chassis number B-0251.

M-type Midget – produced 1928 to 1932
Bodywork: Open and closed 2-str. Engine: 4-cyl, overhead-camshaft, vertical shaft-driven, 57 × 83mm, 847cc, CR 5.4:1, SU carburettor, 20 bhp @ 4,000 rpm, 27 bhp @ 4,500 from 1931. Transmission: 3-speed gearbox, sliding pinion; final drive 4.89:1. Chassis: Wheelbase 6ft 6in, track 3ft 6in; suspension ½-elliptic front and rear with shackles; brakes 8in; wheels bolt-on wire, tyres 3.50 or 4.00 × 19. Chassis numbers M-0251 to M-3485.

C-type Montlhéry Midget – produced 1931 to 1932
Bodywork: Open 2-str. Engine: 4-cyl, overhead-camshaft, vertical shaft-driven, 57 × 73mm, 746cc, 2 SU carburettors or Powerplus blower, 37 bhp @ 6,000 rpm (AA head), 41 bhp @ 6,400 rpm (AB head) or 52.5 bhp @ 6,500 rpm (blower). Transmission: 4-speed gearbox, sliding pinion and remote control; final drive 5.5 or 5.75:1. Chassis: Wheelbase 6ft 9in, track 3ft 6in; suspension ½-elliptic front and rear with sliding trunnions; brakes 8in; wheels bolt-on wire, tyres 3.50 or 4.00 × 19. First Chassis number C-0251.

D-type Midget – produced 1931 to 1932
Bodywork: Open and closed 4-str. Engine: As M-type Midget. Transmission: As M-type except final drive 5.375:1. Chassis: Wheelbase 7ft, later 7ft 2in, track 3ft 6in. Otherwise as C-type. First chassis number D-0500.

F-type Magna – produced 1931 to 1932
Bodywork: Open 2-str, open and closed 4-str. Engine: 6-cyl, overhead-camshaft, vertical shaft-driven, 57 × 83mm, 1,271cc, 2 SU carburettors, 37 bhp @ 4,100 rpm. Transmission: As C-type except final drive 4.78:1 Chassis: Wheelbase 7ft 10in, track 3ft 6in, otherwise as D-type except later cars 12in brakes. Chassis numbers F-0251 to F-1500.

J-type Midget – produced 1932 to 1933 (J1), 1932 to 1934 (J2)
Bodywork: Open 2-str (J2), open and closed 4-str (J1). Engine: As M-type except CR 6.2:1, 2 SU carburettors, 36 bhp @ 5,500 rpm. Transmission: As D-type. Chassis: As later D-type. Chassis numbers (J1) J-0252 to J-0631, (J2) J-0251 and from J-2001.

J3 and J4 Midget – produced 1932 to 1933 (J3), 1933 (J4)
Bodywork: Open 2-str. Engine: As C-type except SU carburettor with Powerplus blower, up to 72 bhp @ 6,000 rpm according to tune. Transmission: As C-type except final drive 4.78:1 (J3) or 5.375:1 (J4). Chassis: As C-type except 8in brakes (J3), 12in brakes (J4), tyres 4.00 × 19 (J3), 4.50 × 19 (J4). Chassis numbers J-3751 to J-3773 (J3), J-4001 to J-4009 (J4).

KA and KB Magnette – produced 1932 to 1933
Bodywork: Open and closed 4-str (K1), open 2-str (K2). Engine: 6-cyl, overhead-camshaft, vertical shaft-driven, 57 × 71mm, 1,087cc, CR 6.4:1, 3 (KA) or 2 (KB) SU carburettors, 39 bhp (KA) or 41 bhp (KB) @ 5,500 rpm. Transmission: 4-speed preselector (KA) or manual (KB) gearbox, final drive 5.78:1. Chassis: Wheelbase 7ft 10in (K2) or 9ft, track 4ft; suspension ½-elliptic front and rear with sliding trunnions; brakes 13in; wheels centre-lock wire, tyres 4.75 × 19. First chassis numbers K-0251 and K2001.

KD and KN Magnette – produced 1933 to 1934
Bodywork: Open 2-str and closed 4-str (K1 and KN). Engine: As KB except 57 × 83mm, 1,271cc, 48.5 or 54.5 (KD) or 56.5 (KN) bhp @ 5,500 rpm. Transmission: 4-speed preselector (KD) or manual (KN) gearbox, final drive 5.78:1. Chassis: As KA and KB Magnette. First chassis numbers K-0322, K-2016 and KN-0251.

K3 Magnette – produced 1932 to 1934
Bodywork: Open 2-str. Engine: As KA/KB except SU carburettor with Marshall or Powerplus blower, CR 6.1:1 std, approx 120 bhp @ 6,500 rpm. Transmission: 4-speed preselector gearbox, final drive 4.33, 4.89 or 5.78:1. Chassis: As KA/KB (K2). Chassis numbers K-3751 and K3001 to K-3031.

L-type Magna – produced 1933 to 1934
Bodywork: Open 2-str (L2), open and closed 4-str (L1). Engine: As KB Magnette. Transmission: As KB Magnette except final drive 5.375:1. Chassis: As K2 Magnette except track 3ft 6in, brakes 12in, tyres 4.50 × 19. First chassis number L-0251, L2 from L-2001 to L-2090.

P-type Midget – produced 1934 to 1935 (PA), 1935 to 1936 (PB)
Bodywork: Open 2-str and 4-str, closed 2-str. Engine: 4-cyl, overhead-camshaft, vertical shaft-driven, 57 × 83mm (PA), 60 × 83mm (PB), 847cc (PA), 939cc (PB), CR 6.1:1 (PA), 6.8:1 (PB), 2 SU carburettors, 36 bhp (PA), 43 bhp (PB) @ 5,500 rpm. Transmission: 4-speed gearbox, sliding pinion and remote control; final drive 5.375:1. Chassis: Wheelbase 7ft 3¼in, track 3ft 6in, suspension ½-elliptic front and rear with sliding trunnions; brakes 12in; wheels centre-lock wire, tyres 4.00 × 19. Chassis numbers PA-0251 to PA-2250 and from PB-0251.

NA, NB, ND and NE Magnette – produced 1934 to 1936
Bodywork: Open 2-str (NA, NB, ND and NE) and open 4-str (NA, NB). Engine: NA, NB and ND as KD Magnette except 56.5 bhp @ 5,500 rpm, NE CR 9.5:1, 74 bhp @ 6,500 rpm. Transmission: As KB Magnette except final drive 5.125:1 or 4.875:1 (NE). Chassis: As KB Magnette except wheelbase 8ft, track 3ft 9in, brakes 12in, tyres 4.75 × 18. Chassis numbers NA-0251 to NA-0995, (NE numbers NA-0516 to NA-0522).

Q-type Midget – produced 1934
Bodywork: Open 2-str. Engine: 4-cyl, overhead-camshaft, vertical shaft-driven, 57 × 73mm, 746cc, CR 6.4:1, SU carburettor with Zoller blower, 113 bhp @ 7,200 rpm. Transmission: 4-speed preselector gearbox, final drive 4.5:1 or 4.875:1. Chassis: Wheelbase 7ft 10in, track 3ft 9in; suspension ½-elliptic front and rear with sliding trunnions; brakes 12in; wheels centre-lock wire, tyres 4.75 × 18. Chassis numbers QA-0251 to QA-0258.

R-type Midget – produced 1935
Bodywork: Open single-seater. Engine: As Q-type Midget. Transmission: As Q-type Midget. Chassis: As Q-type Midget except wheelbase 7ft 6½in. Chassis numbers RA-0251 to RA-0260.

TA and TB Midget – produced 1936 to 1939 (TA) and 1939 (TB)
Bodywork: Open 2-str and closed 2-str (TA). Engine: 4-cyl, overhead-valve, 63.5 × 102mm (TA), 66.5 × 90mm (TB), 1,292cc (TA), 1,250cc (TB), CR 6.5:1 (TA), 7.3:1 (TB), 2 SU carburettors, 50 bhp @ 4,500 rpm (TA), 54 bhp @ 5,200 rpm (TB). Transmission: 4-speed gearbox, final drive 4.875:1 (TA), 5.12:1 (TB). Chassis: Wheelbase 7ft 10in, track 3ft 9in; suspension ½-elliptic front and rear with sliding trunnions; brakes 9in hydraulic; wheels centre-lock wire, tyres 4.50 × 19. Chassis numbers TA-0251 to TA-3253 and TB-0251 to TB-0629.

SA 2-litre – produced 1936 to 1939
Bodywork: Open and closed 4-str. Engine: 6-cyl, overhead-valve, initially 69 × 102mm, 2,288cc, then 69.5 × 102mm, 2,322 cc, CR 6.5:1, 2 SU carburettors, 78 bhp @ 4,200 rpm. Transmission: 4-speed gearbox, final drive 4.75:1 Chassis: Wheelbase 10ft 3in, track 4ft 5½in; suspension ½-elliptic front and rear with shackles; brakes 12in hydraulic; wheels centre-lock wire, tyres 5.50 × 18. Chassis numbers SA-0251 to SA-2988.

VA 1½-litre – produced 1937 to 1939
Bodywork: Open and closed 4-str. Engine: 4-cyl, overhead-valve, 69.5 × 102mm, 1,548cc, CR 6.5:1,2 SU carburettors, 55 bhp @ 4,400 rpm. Transmission: 4-speed gearbox, final drive 5.22:1. Chassis: Wheelbase 9ft, track 4ft 2in; suspension ½-elliptic front and rear with shackles; brakes 10in hydraulic; wheels centre-lock wire, tyres 5.00 × 19. Chassis numbers VA-0251 to VA-2657.

WA 2.6-litre – produced 1938 to 1939
Bodywork: Open and closed 4-str. Engine: 6-cyl, overhead-valve, 73 × 102mm, 2,561cc, CR 7.3:1, 2 SU carburettors, 95 bhp @ 4,400 rpm. Transmission: 4-speed gearbox, final drive 4.78:1. Chassis: As SA 2-litre except rear track 4ft 8¾in, brakes 14in hydraulic. Chassis numbers WA-0251 to WA-0619.

TC Midget – produced 1945 to 1949
Bodywork: Open 2-str. Engine: As TB Midget except optional CR 7.5:1. Transmission: As TB Midget. Chassis: As TB Midget. Chassis numbers TC-0251 to TC-10252.

Y-type 1¼-litre – produced 1947 to 1953
Bodywork: Closed 4-str (YT) and closed 4-str (YA, YB). Engine: As TC Midget except 1 SU carburettor, 46 bhp @ 4,800 rpm (YA, YB). Transmission: As TC Midget except final drive 5.14:1. Chassis: Wheelbase 8ft 3in, track 3ft 11½in front, 4ft 2in rear; suspension independent coil front, ½-elliptic with shackles rear; brakes 9in hydraulic; wheels bolt-on disc, tyres 5.25 × 16. First chassis numbers Y-0251, YB-0251 and YT-0251.

TD Midget – produced 1949 to 1953
Bodywork: Open 2-str. Engine: As TC Midget except CR 7.25:1. Transmission: As TC Midget. Chassis: Wheelbase 7ft 10in, track 3ft 11½in front, 4ft 2in rear; tyres 5.50 × 16, otherwise as Y-type 1¼-litre. Chassis numbers TD-0251 to TD-9158 (TD) and TD-9159 to TD-29915 (TD II).

TF Midget – produced 1953 to 1954
Bodywork: Open 2-str. Engine: TF 1250 as TC Midget except CR 8:1, 57 bhp @ 5,500 rpm, TF 1500 as TC Midget except 72 × 90mm, 1,466cc, CR 8.3:1, 63 bhp @ 5,000 rpm. Transmission: As TC Midget except final drive 4.875:1. Chassis: As TD Midget except optional centre-lock wire wheels. Chassis numbers TF-0501 to TF-6500, TF-6651 to TF-6750 and TF-6851 to TF-6950 (TF 1250) and TF-6501 to TF-6650, TF-6751 to TF-6850 and TF-6951 to TF-10100 (TF 1500).

ZA and ZB Magnette – produced 1953 to 1956
Bodywork: Closed 4-str. Engine: 4-cyl, overhead-valve, 73 × 89mm, 1,489cc, CR 7.15:1 (ZA), 8.3:1 (ZB), 2 SU carburettors, 60 bhp @ 4,600 rpm (ZA), 68 bhp @ 5,250 rpm (ZB). Transmission: As TF Midget. Chassis: Wheelbase 8ft 6in, track 4ft 3in; suspension independent coil front, ½-elliptic rear; brakes 10in hydraulic; wheels bolt-on disc, tyres 5.50 × 15. First chassis numbers ZA-0501 and ZB-18101.

MGA 1500 – produced 1955 to 1959
Bodywork: Open and closed 2-str. Engine: As ZB Magnette except initially 68 bhp @ 5,500 rpm, then 72 bhp @ 5,500 rpm. Transmission: 4-speed gearbox, final drive 4.1:1, 4.3:1 or 4.5:1. Chassis: Wheelbase 7ft 10in, track 3ft 11½in front, 4ft 0¾in rear; brakes 10in hydraulic; tyres 5.60 × 15, otherwise as TF Midget. Chassis numbers 10101 to 68850.

MGA 1600 – produced 1959 to 1962
Bodywork: Open and closed 2-str. Engine: As MGA 1500 except 75.4 × 89mm, 1,588cc (Mk I), 76 × 89mm, 1,622cc (Mk II), CR 8.3:1 (Mk I), 8.9:1 (Mk II), 79.5 bhp @ 5,600 rpm (Mk I), 93 bhp @ 5,500 rpm (Mk II). Transmission: As MGA 1500 except final drive 4.3:1 (Mk I), 4.1:1 (Mk II). Chassis: As MGA 1500 except brakes 11in disc front (Mk II). Chassis numbers 68851 to 100351 (Mk I) and 100352 to 109070 (Mk II).

MGA Twin Cam – produced 1958 to 1960
Bodywork: Open and closed 2-str. Engine: As MGA 1600 Mk I except twin overhead camshafts, CR 9.9:1, 108 bhp @ 6,700 rpm. Transmission: As MGA 1600 Mk I. Chassis: As MGA 1600 except front track 3ft 11.9in; brakes 10¾in discs front and rear; wheels centre-lock ventilated disc, tyres 5.90 × 15. Chassis numbers 501 to 2611.

Magnette – produced 1959 to 1961 (Mk III), 1961 to 1968 (Mk IV)
Bodywork: Closed 4-str. Engine: Mk III as ZB Magnette except 66.5 bhp @ 5,200 rpm, Mk IV as MGA 1600 MK II

except 68 bhp @ 5,000 rpm. Transmission: As ZB Magnette except three-speed automatic optional on Mk IV, final drive 4.3:1. Chassis: Mk III wheelbase 8ft 3¼in, track 4ft 0½in front, 4ft 2in rear, Mk IV wheelbase 8ft 4½in, track 4ft 2½in front, 4ft 3½in rear; suspension independent coil front, ½-elliptic rear; brakes 9in hydraulic; wheels bolt-on disc, tyres 5.90 × 14. Abingdon chassis numbers inapplicable as cars built elsewhere.

MG 1100 and MG 1300 – produced 1962 to 1971
Bodywork: Closed 4-str. Engine: 4-cyl, overhead-valve, 64.6 × 84mm, 1,098cc, CR 8.9:1, 2 SU carburettors, 56 bhp @ 5,500 rpm (1100), 70.6 × 81.3mm, 1,275cc, CR 8.8:1, 1 SU carburettor, 58 bhp @ 5,250 rpm (1300). Transmission: 4-speed gearbox, 4-speed automatic optional on 1300, final drive 4.1:1 (1100), 3.64:1 (1300). Chassis: Wheelbase 7ft 9½in, track 4ft 3½in front, 4ft 3in rear; suspension independent Hydrolastic front and rear; brakes 8in, disc front drum rear; wheels bolt-on disc, tyres 5.50 × 12. Abingdon chassis numbers inapplicable as cars built elsewhere.

Midget Mk I – produced 1961 to 1964
Bodywork: Open 2-str. Engine: 4-cyl, overhead-valve, G-AN1 series 63 × 76mm, 948cc, CR 9:1 or 8.3:1, 46 bhp @ 5,500 rpm, G-AN2 series 64.6 × 84mm, 1,098cc, CR 8.9:1 or 8.1:1, 56 bhp @ 5,500 rpm, 2 SU carburettors. Transmission: 4-speed gearbox, final drive 4.22:1. Chassis: Wheelbase 6ft 8in, track 3ft 9¾in front, 3ft 8¾in rear; suspension independent coil front, ¼-elliptic rear; brakes 7in hydraulic, G-AN2 8¼in discs front; wheels bolt-on disc, centre-lock wire optional on G-AN2, tyres 5.20 × 13. Chassis numbers G-AN1-101 to G-AN1-16183 and G-AN2-16184 to G-AN2-25787.

Midget MK II – produced 1964 to 1966
Bodywork: Open 2-str. Engine: As Midget Mk I G-AN2 series except CR 9.1:1 or 8.9:1, 59 bhp @ 5,750 rpm. Transmission: As Midget Mk I. Chassis: As Midget Mk I except suspension ½-elliptic rear, brakes as G-AN2. Chassis numbers G-AN3-25788 to G-AN3-52389.

Midget Mk III and Mk IV – produced 1966 to 1974
Bodywork: Open 2-str. Engine: 4-cyl, overhead-valve, 70.6 × 81.3mm, 1,275cc, CR 8.8:1 or 8:1, 2 SU carburettors, 65 bhp @ 6,000 rpm. Transmission: As Midget Mk II except final drive changed to 3.9:1 during production of Mk IV (G-AN5 series). Chassis: As Midget Mk II except bolt-on ribbed steel wheels adopted during production, tyres 145SR-13. Chassis numbers G-AN4-52390 to G-AN4-74885 and G-AN5-74886 to G-AN5-153920.

Midget MK IV 1500 – produced 1974 to 1979
Bodywork: Open 2-str. Engine: 4-cyl, overhead-valve, 73.7 × 87.5mm, 1,493cc, CR 9:1, 2 SU carburettors, 66 bhp @ 5,500 rpm. Transmission: 4-speed gearbox, final drive 3.9:1. Chassis: As Mk IV except track 3ft 10½in front, 3ft 9in rear. Chassis numbers G-AN6-154101 to G-AN6-229526.

MGB and MGB GT – produced 1962 to 1980
Bodywork: Open and closed 2-str. Engine: 4-cyl, overhead-valve, 80.3 × 89mm, 1,798cc, CR 8.8:1, 2 SU carburettors, 95 bhp @ 5,400 rpm. Engine specification repeatedly changed to suit different market requirements and legislation during course of production. Transmission: 4-speed gearbox, optional overdrive, final drive 3.9:1. Chassis: Wheelbase 7ft 7in, track 4ft 1in front, 4ft 1¼in rear; suspension independent coil front, ½-elliptic rear; brakes 10¾in discs front, 10in drums rear; wheels bolt-on disc, optional centre-lock wire, tyres 5.60 × 14, later 155-14 and 165-14. Chassis numbers 101 to 218651, 219000 to 256646, 258001 to 294987, 295301 to 327990, 328101 to 360069, 360301 to 367818, 367901 to 386267, 386601 to 409400, 410001 to 444499 and 447001 to 523002.

MGC and MGC GT – produced 1967 to 1969
Bodywork: Open and closed 2-str. Engine: 6-cyl, overhead valve, 83.3 × 89mm, displacement 2,912cc, CR 9:1, 2 SU carburettors, 145 bhp @ 5,250 rpm. Transmission: 4-speed gearbox, optional overdrive, final drive 3.07:1, 3.31:1 with overdrive. Chassis: As MGB except track 4ft 2in front, 4ft 1½in rear; suspension independent torsion bar front; brakes 11in discs front, 9in drums rear; tyres 165-15. Chassis numbers 101 to 9102.

MGB GT V8 – produced 1973 to 1976
Bodywork: Closed 2-str. Engine: V8-cyl, overhead valve, 89 × 71mm, 3,528cc, CR 8.25:1, 2 SU carburettors, 137 bhp @ 5,000 rpm. Transmission: 4-speed gearbox with overdrive, final drive 3.07:1. Chassis: As MGB GT except wheels bolt-on disc, tyres 175HR-14. Chassis numbers 101 to 2903.

Total production of MG cars
(Quantities quoted are estimations or approximations where definitive records no longer exist.)

11.9	6
14/28 Super Sports	400
14/28 and 14/40 Mk IV	900
18/80 Mk I and Mk II	736
18/80 Six Mk III	5
M-type Midget	3,235
C-type Midget	44
D-type Midget	250
F-type Magna	1,250
J1 and J2 Midget	2,463
J3 and J4 Midget	31
KA and KB Magnette	86
KD and KN Magnette	286
K3 Magnette	33
L-type Magna	576
P-type Midget	2,526
N-type Magnette	745
Q-type Midget	8
R-type Midget	10
TA and TB Midget	3,382
SA 2-litre	2,738
VA 1½-litre	2,407
WA 2.6-litre	369
TC Midget	10,000
Y-type 1¼-litre	8.336
TD Midget	29,664
TF Midget	9,600
ZA and ZB Magnette	36,600
MGA 1500	58,750
MGA 1600	40,220
MGA Twin Cam	2,111
Magnette Mk III and IV	29,414
MG 1100 and 1300	143,000
Midget Mk I	25,681
Midget Mk II	26,601
Midget Mk III and IV	100,345
Midget Mk IV 1500	73,899
MGB and MGB GT	513,272
MGC and MGC GT	8,999
MGB GT V8	2,591

The famous octagon, one of the best known and most widely respected corporate symbols throughout the world of cars, has been carried with honour by MGs for more than half a century. Sports cars, saloons, coupes and even single-seater record-breakers, they have all been endowed with that extra ingredient — a combination of flair and highly developed fitness for purpose — which has been such an enduring characteristic of the products of Abingdon. The following pictorial tribute is a reminder of a segment of British automobile history which can never be emulated and which will remain a source of pride for as long as cars are admired and enjoyed.

The Morris Oxford was soundly designed and built — advantages not universally available amongst light cars in 1914, when Cowley offered a Sporting Model on a 'Specially picked and tuned De Luxe chassis'. The single-seater cost £220 'fully equipped with three lamps'.

Another MG ancestor, the Morris Garages-built tourer on a Morris Silent Six F-type chassis, with side-valve 2,320-cc engine giving 39 bhp at 2,800 rpm. All the Kimber features are there. Unfortunately, the long crankshaft lacked effective torsional vibration damping.

Jack Gardiner, of the Morris Garages staff, ordered a car similar to this polished aluminium four-seater pictured in June 1924 on location in North Oxford. The type went into production as the first of the Pusey Lane cars to wear the MG octagon. The side-valve engine gave 30 bhp from its 1,802 cc and was mounted in the Oxford 8-ft 6-in wheelbase chassis, which had rear brakes only. The opening three-piece windscreen is devoid of wipers.

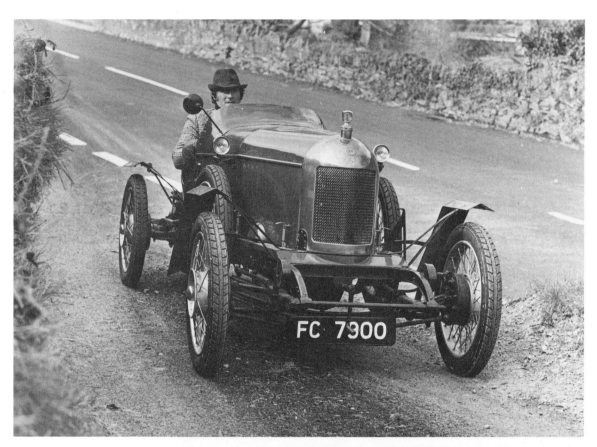

The first true MG sports car and always celebrated as such by Cecil Kimber, who had it built for his own use, the Kimber Special was built to take part in the 1925 Lands End long-distance trial, in which it won a gold medal. The car revisited its old haunts in 1974 for these location pictures and is seen at the beginning of and climbing Beggars Roost.

51

The Kimber Special's engine shortly after the company had re-acquired the car. It had been involved in an accident on December 12, 1932, and now was fitted with cycle-type wings and a vee screen.

The 1925 two-seater tourer. These famous pictures, taken in March that year, provided the reference material for contemporary magazine and brochure illustrations. The rear dickey seat was a single and the car was priced at £350.

A close-up view of the interior of the 1925 two-seater. Note the right-handed handbrake, which was a widely used feature at that time.

The 14/28 two-seater tourer with front-wheel brakes pictured in the yard of the old Cowley military academy. There is still an opening screen, but a wiper was available from 1925. Outside door handles are fitted and the upper part of the body is steel-panelled. Miles Thomas drove one of these cars for a year and reported at length on his experiences in *The Morris Owner* in 1926. The painted numberplates cost just 15s (75p).

A 1927 14/28 tourer pictured outside the Palace of Westminster. A valance has been added to the smaller Cowley radiator to make the car look lower-slung. No fan was provided on these engines and the drive was used to power the windscreen wiper. Amongst the chassis modifications was the removal of the rubber mounting pad for the steering box to give more responsive steering. The Morris Oxford badge has been supplemented by the MG octagon. The bolt-on Magna wheels could be covered by Ace discs at a cost of £4.10s (£4.50) for a set of five.

The radiator valance was discarded after 1927, as illustrated, a year later, by this Mark IV Salonette. The interior of the same car reveals that much use was made of the octagon theme — a feature of Kimber's taste to the end of his car-building days. The white-faced Watford instruments are particularly appealing. Note the Barker headlamp dipper lever alongside the handbrake. Built on the 8-ft 10½-in wheelbase chassis, the Mark IV was quoted as producing 35 bhp — the first time the output had differed from the standard Morris rating.

Based on an abortive Morris Light Six of 1927, from which it inherited its narrow 4-ft track, the Mark I chassis was equipped with a long-stroke chain-driven overhead-camshaft engine, which later found its way into the Isis. Built in part to MG's requirements, the 2,468-cc engine had a compression ratio of 5.75:1 and drove via a three-speed gearbox to a 4.25:1 rear axle. Announced at the 1928 London Motor Show and publicized by this superb show chassis, the car carried the definitive MG radiator. Its rocker cover was cut away to reveal the ingenious L-shaped rocker arms and slightly inclined valves.

The Mark I Salonette. Far less appealing than earlier open cars, these were built at a time when British closed-car design was not strong. The short bonnet section and the stumpy boot didn't help.

The Mark I Salonette which Sir Francis Samuelson drove in the 1929 Monte Carlo Rally, starting from John O'Groats. He was third fastest in the *Mont des Mules* hill-climb and took a special award in the coachwork competition. The car is fitted with bolt-on wheels and was exhibited at the 1928 London Motor Show.

The interior of the Mark I as road-tested by *The Motor* early in 1929. There is a British Berkshire electric windscreen wiper and the instruments were described as 'artistically grouped'.

The same car on test by *The Motor.* They found that it weighed 1 ton 9 cwt, the four-door body clearly weighing more than that of the Salonette. A top speed of 78 mph was recorded, with 55 mph in third gear. Overall fuel consumption was 18/20 mpg.

Although the Salonette was close-coupled, the deep footwells provided rear passengers of the Mark I with adequate space, while the high-mounted centre armrest gave useful lateral support.

The standard-bodied Mark I open four-seater tourer, which was provided with a small luggage boot. The rear wings encroached considerably on the lower part of the doors.

A Mark I chassis in course of show preparation. The battery-box structure amidships was designed to give some stiffening without the restriction on rear passenger foot space imposed by full-scale cruciform bracing, later adopted by some marques.

A Mark II show engine. A revised breather was fitted to the rocker cover and the neat polished covers were necessary in front of the block since the MG version of the Morris Motors Engine Branch unit didn't use the fan of the standard version. The bulkhead-mounted oil header tank contained 2 gallons.

Mark I chassis production under way at Edmund Road in May 1929. MG's assembly method was destined never to change fundamentally down the years.

A show Mark II chassis. The remote control for the new four-speed gearbox is a feature and the exhaust manifold is cut away to reveal the smooth passage for gases. The chassis lubrication reservoir is mounted on the bulkhead and the springs are set nearly flat. The wider lateral spring base and the extra 4 inches of track materially improved roadholding.

The Mark II chassis lent itself to flights of fancy such as this two-seater with aircraft and yachting motifs. The rear decking could be lifted to accept a hood.

Mark I production overlapped that of the Mark II in 1930 and this metal-panelled four-door saloon is typical of production closed cars of the period.

Rows of Mark II engines awaiting installation at Abingdon.

A Mark I saloon on test in a quiet booth with a stethoscope being used to identify an elusive tap.

The raised deck of the Mark II two-seater illustrated on the previous page. This attention to detail is typical of the care given to bodies of cars in the £600 price bracket at the time.

The final-preparation bay at Abingdon with a four-door Mark II saloon equipped with the optional radiator stoneguard followed by a couple of M-type Midgets in April 1930.

A new era arrived with the Morris Minor of 1928. Despite its half-elliptic springs, overhead-camshaft 850-cc engine and four-wheel brakes, it was never as profitable as its rival, the Austin 7, but it provided Kimber with a tiny best-seller.

A fabric-bodied Midget in original production form. The brake cables are carried outside the body, while the door hinges are to the rear. It was tested in this form by *The Motor* in July 1930, when it weighed 10 cwt 20 lb unladen, recorded a top speed of 65 mph (42 mph in second) and cost £175.

The M-type's oval dash panel was simplicity itself, with dials for speed, oil pressure and amperes. No windscreen wiper was in evidence on this or the road-test car.

An M-type engine installed in a D-type chassis in August 1931. The vertical drive to the overhead camshaft was to be a consistent MG feature. Accessibility was always good on these cars and continued to be a pre-occupation with MG's engineers.

A picture gallery of the M-type, the first of an illustrious line of Midgets. An early chassis, seen on the right, was virtually standard Minor. Its 6-ft 6-in wheelbase endowed the car with a characteristically pitchy ride. The miniscule brakes. which included one on the transmission, are noteworthy. The completed car is one of the later versions, photographed at the end of 1929 and featuring brake lever within the bodywork, no transmission brake and front-mounted doors. Windscreen wipers are still not in evidence, however.

An early production line for the M-type at Edmund Road, before the move to Abingdon. The gravity-fed fuel tank can be seen mounted on the bulkhead behind the engine.

The front axle and brake assembly of an M-type, with a friction-type shock absorber just visible.

An M-type Midget coupe photographed in December 1929. This fabric-bodied example, with a particularly neat bonnet treatment, was purely a two-seater, with plenty of boot space, but it was not put into production.

A luncheon was held in January 1930 to celebrate the opening of the Abingdon factory. Present were Sir Francis Samuelson (right), Sir William Morris, Cecil Kimber and (left) E. McCormick, co-driver to Samuelson when he drove this Mark II in the 1930 Monte Carlo Rally.

A vertically slatted radiator was made available for the Mark II.

The standard four-door saloon in De Luxe form, its lines enhanced considerably by the contrasting colour of the wheels. The screen wipers are mounted from the base of the screen, whereas on the Monte Carlo Rally car at the top of the page they are top-mounted.

Road-tested by *The Motor* in June 1930, this Mark II two-seater tackled the Lands End trial in the course of a 2,000-miles appraisal. It recorded 72 mph at Brooklands and, at the end of the test, 78.26 mph over the flying half-mile. Top gear was 4.27:1 and third a usefully high 5.58:1. Built on the 9-ft 6-in wheelbase chassis, the car weighed 37 cwt 3 lb.

In 1930, an M-type climbed the Beggars Roost trials hill 100 times without stopping the engine. Although the car was prepared with a rear-mounted spare wheel to aid traction it was not needed. Here it is about to make another climb.

The very neat £245 M-type coupe, which measured 54 inches high and was offered in either black or grey, with the wings and chassis in black, and with a choice of blue, red, green or grey leather interior.

Rear view of the same car, the sliding roof of which has three transparent panels.

Interior of an M-type coupe. The cranked gearlever for the three-speed gearbox and the inaccessible handbrake are evident. The steering column is adjustable for rake and the door is provided with cutaways for the driver's elbow and a cubby hole.

The bucket seats for the front passengers of the coupe folded forward to provide access to the rear seat and its deep footwells. The back squab and cushion were readily detachable and the space could be used for a travelling trunk.

The M-types made a great impression in the 1930 Double Twelve race at Brooklands, where in this scene the Randall/Montgomery and Stisted/Black cars climb the banking out of the finishing straight. Black put in one lap at 72.45 mph and the cars won the team prize after finishing third and fourth in their class. Replicas were offered at £245 and 18 were sold.

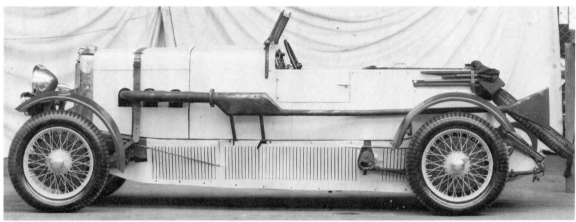

The Mark III 18/100 made its racing debut in the same event. With a top gear of 3.6:1 (third was 4.7:1) it was capable of 110 mph at approximately 4,600 rpm. The deep valance along the body gives the car a clumsy appearance, but was necessary to support the undershield.

One of the most purposeful front views of any vintage car. The roughness of Brooklands dictated the massive girder construction for the mudguards and headlamps, and the body and screen were built to meet international regulations.

The massive front brakes of the Mark III were cable-operated, while the Dunlop tyres were stamped 29 x 5-00 on their sidewalls.

This is the standard rear axle, fuel tank and shock absorber layout for a Mark II chassis.

The Mark III rear-end, with extra dampers and fuel tanks slung low in front of the axle. The standard chassis height of 18 inches was lowered by flattening the springs.

The crossflow cylinder-head of the 18/100 was fed by twin downdraught SU carburettors. Based on the Isis engine, but fitted with a dry sump, the engine was intended to give 100 bhp and more than 100 mph, but it proved reluctant to sustain this output for more than a short period.

The three-branch exhaust of the 18/100 dry-sump engine. There is a strong family resemblance between this and later six-cylinder engines.

Rear view of the Mark III 18/100 sports four-seater, in this instance equipped with Avon tyres and without any valance concealing the underpan. Altogether five of these cars were built.

The earlier Mark I chassis was proving difficult to sell, and a new six-cylinder Speed Model, based on the three-speed Mark I, was announced. With striking fabric-covered open touring body it weighed only 22 cwt 93 lb.

The Speed Model, which was road-tested to a top speed of 80.36 mph and 61.22 mph in second, proved so flexible that top could be held down to 5 mph. The brakes were Dewandre servo-assisted, and at £525 the car cost the same as the standard tourer.

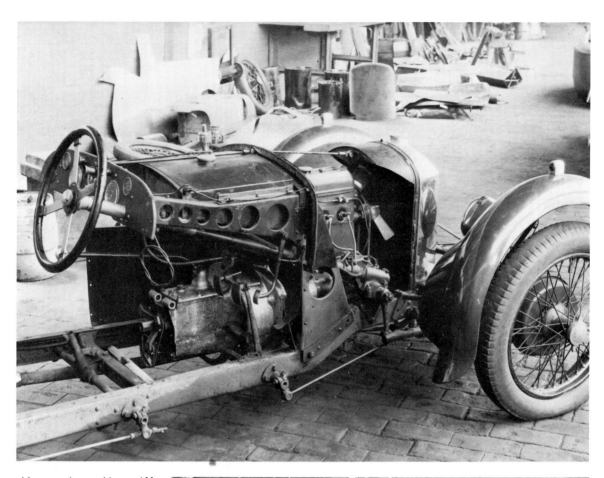

After experience with tuned M-types it was clear that MG's future was with small sports cars, so Abingdon looked around for inspiration. The French Rally was a simple, robust and stable car, so one was bought and stripped. Features adopted included the underslung chassis, tubular rear crossmember and centre-lock wire wheels. The layshaft by the gearbox is for the speedometer drive, and note the ribbed rear brakes. Fortunately, the long cranked gearlever was not copied, but the simple bulkhead and the upsweep of the front of the chassis were to become Abingdon features.

By 1931, the Mark II drophead two-seater had developed into a handsome car. Variations in specification were still possible, this example having a side-mounted spare wheel on the left. The car cost £625.

The four-seater drophead was a neat design, without the outside hood irons and with 'English-school' swept wings rather than the fashionable French-influenced helmet wings of the other cars.

A similar car, but without the side-mounted spare. Twin windscreen wipers are fitted and the small golf bag locker behind the passenger's door is neatly executed.

A Brunell picture of a Mark I
Speed Model driven by the
photographer's daughter Kitty
at a West Country ford.
Although his need to meet
deadlines meant that he often
shot a picture in less than ideal
conditions, Brunell had a keen
eye for the design of a
landscape.

A brace of M-types in the idyllic
setting of the South Downs
during an early-1930s Brighton-
Beer trial. Brunell took this
evocative picture with an eye
to classic rules of composition.

MG Mark I and Midget models nearing completion on two parallel assembly lines at Abingdon in January 1930.

A carefully restored M-type engine. The only 'error' is the vertical loop in the petrol pipe, regarded by old-school engineers as conducive to air locks.

Even in 1932 the local registration number JO 1 was cherished, and this M-type Midget is bearing it proudly during an MCC Buxton trial. The JO and RX prefixes were to become well-known, identifying cars in which the works had an interest, either for competition and development, or for the press fleet.

A Mark II chassis on the Comparator after having been tested. Behind is an M-type on a simpler roller test, and a Mark I chassis and a saloon can be seen amongst a selection of Midgets in the background. This photograph provided the reference material for the well-known Gordon Crosby illustration of the MG factory.

Engines on test at Abingdon, with an M-type unit in the foreground and a six-cylinder receiving attention behind it.

Jarvis, the Surrey-based MG distributors, built this attractive occasional four-seater on the M-type chassis. Ducellier headlamps are fitted.

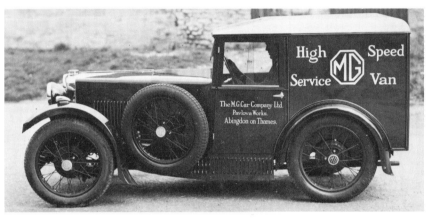

This high-speed delivery van, dating from 1931, was a modified M-type Midget with the payload poised neatly over the back axle.

The lessons learnt from the Rally were put to good use in EX 120, seen here at Brooklands with a worried-looking Cousins, Jackson and Eyston (in the cockpit) in March 1931, when the flying-mile and flying-kilometre records were taken at 97 mph. However, the car was under par, having taken the first-ever 750-cc class records at over 100 mph the previous month at Montlhéry. The front axle was still M-type, but it carried Rudge Whitworth centre-lock wheels.

The EX 120 and the production supercharged C-type chassis were displayed at a luncheon held at Abingdon in March 1931 to celebrate the 100-mph records. Amongst those present, from left to right, are Hicks, Earl Howe, the Earl of March, Kimber, Denly, McConnell, Horton, Cousins, Charles, Jackson and Propert. The low chassis, rear-mounted fuel tank and SU carburettor dashpot to the right of the radiator can be seen on the C-type chassis.

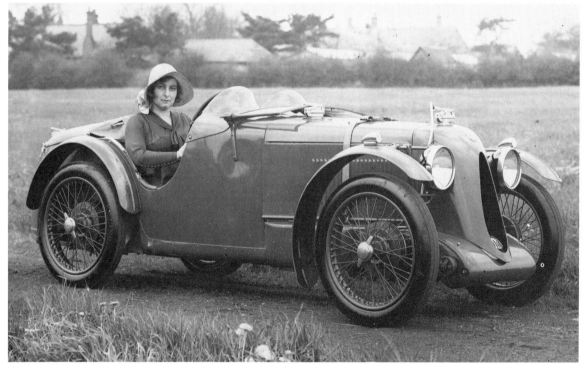

The Hon Mrs Chetwynd pictured in her party frock in a C-type. The almost plain racing tyres were necessary wear for Brooklands. Note the quick-release fillers on the radiator and bonnet tops, also the sturdy strap securing the engine cover. The C-type was equipped with a particularly neat remote-control gearlever.

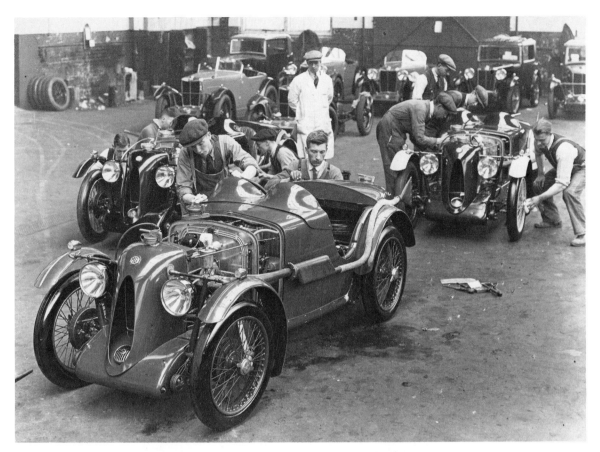

A fleet of C-types being prepared in double-quick time for the 1931 JCC Double Twelve race, the whole programme being completed in a matter of weeks, even though the cars were prepared to the most meticulous standard. Note the armoured wiring and the elbow pad for the mechanic on the car in the foreground. The cars were fitted with undershields.

An M-type with a Powerplus blower similar to that of the C-type. The blower cost an extra £20 and blew at 8 to 10 psi. The large-bore inlet pipe was bypassed at idling speeds, a smaller-section pipe coming in to obviate lumpy running. A four-speed gearbox was a recommended fitment at £50 extra, and clearly Abingdon was thinking of blown engines for road use at this period.

C-type Midgets at the pits at Brooklands prior to the 1931 JCC Double Twelve race. The Earl of March's winning car, number 60, averaged 65.6 mph.

Drivers run for their cars at the start of the second day's race. Cousins, responsible for the Earl of March's team, elected to run the cars at undiminished speed that day and avoided the valve troubles which afflicted other cars.

Dan Higgins swoops on to the finishing straight, lapping in excess of 70 mph and well ahead of the other C-types, before retiring on the first afternoon.

80

Crammed into the small cockpit, the Earl of March's mechanic glances over his shoulder while his driver concentrates on the road ahead.

A new record-breaker appeared at Montlhéry in September 1931. EX 127 was built to have a minimal cross-section and the transmission was offset by 6 degrees to allow the driver to sit low beside the propeller-shaft.

After engine-cooling problems due to a bulky chain-and-sprocket blower drive in front of the engine, Eldridge installed a surface radiator and took the 5-kilometre 750-class record at 110.28 mph before radiator trouble intervened.

Shortly before Christmas 1931, Eyston returned to Montlhéry with EX 127 and a new blower drive and took the 10-kilometre record at 114 mph. The radiator was partly blanked-off.

Despite all its record-breaking achievements, EX 127, the Magic Midget, never managed to win a race in Britain. Here it is during the 1932 500-Miles race at Brooklands, where it was driven by Eyston and Denly until it retired.

EX 127, with Eyston aboard, being eased down on to the sands at Pendine for the early-1931 record attempts. Troubles with the timing equipment prevented satisfactory results in the time available. Hand timing gave the car a one-way run at 122 mph, but the best recorded officially was at 119.5 mph.

The neat remote-control selector gate for the gearbox of the F-type Magna. Note also the accessible fly-off handbrake with an adjuster at its base.

The F-type Magna chassis with a 1,271-cc engine derived via the M-type Midget from a Wolseley design. The trunnion sliding mounting at the end of the rear spring and the small brakes can be seen.

In 1935, EX 127 went to the German driver Kohlrausch. It was fitted with a Q-type engine and Zoller blower giving some 146 bhp, and with a version of the narrow body originally built for Denly it covered the flying-mile on the Frankfurt autobahn at 140.6 mph.

An early D-type, possibly the prototype car, with the tiny four-seater bodywork which was to spoil handling when fully laden. Cheapness was evidently in the designer's mind, and the car sold for £210. The 850-cc Midget engine was coupled to a three-speed gearbox with remote control.

The cockpit of the D-type four-seater, the chassis and gearchange of which was derived from the C-type. The speedometer, flanked by the oil pressure gauge and the ammeter, carries both total and trip mileage recordings.

The F-type foursome coupe, otherwise known as the 12/70 hp Magna Six, was introduced in September 1931. In the manner of the time, the long bonnet hinted at a much more ambitious installation than the 1,271-cc engine found there. The car cost £289 with a sliding roof.

The F1 sports four-seater shared the low chassis — 11 inches from the ground — of the coupe, but was something of a sheep in wolf's clothing with its 37 bhp, 8-inch brakes and 4.89:1 gearing with a maximum of 4,100 rpm.

The F1 coupe had the same instrument panel as the D-type. Economy was very much the keynote in these models, which sold well.

The six-cylinder F1 engine was given cosmetic attention to ensure it did not resemble the Wolseley Hornet from which it was derived.

Cecil Kimber in his office at Abingdon. The Magic Midget ornament was to be expected, but the 'leaping jaguar' mascot looks curiously familiar and was also to be found on one of the 18/100 sports models.

A close-up picture of the Magic Midget model on Kimber's desk.

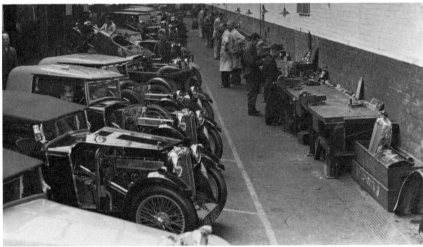

A metal-panelled M-type Midget with the hood erect, but without sidescreens. There still seems to be no provision for a wiper. M-type production finished in 1932.

The Abingdon service bay with a line of F-type Magna coupes much in evidence and a Midget hoisted to receive front-end attention.

The engine-build bay in April 1932, with an F-type six-cylinder unit receiving attention in the foreground. Note the octagonal panels over the engine test beds. The long-lasting policy of showing MG owners around the plant had already been established.

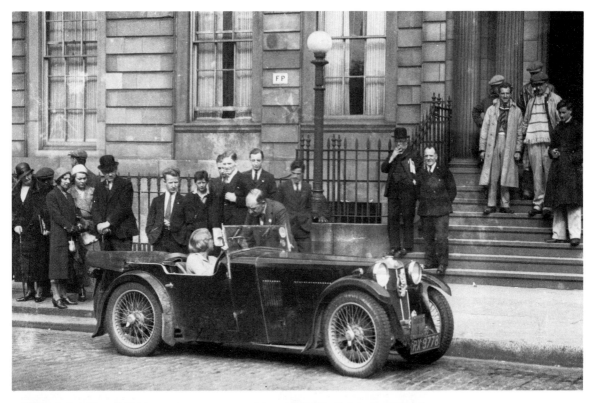

This 1932 F1 Magna was the first car away at the start of the Scottish Rally, driven by Kitty Brunell. Note how the gathering of interested spectators range from the bowler-hatted to the trench-coated motorcyclists on the steps.

A pair of blown C-types in the 1932 Ulster TT, which was not a happy race for the type. The cars show the close approximation to the later J-type body after a larger fuel tank had become necessary to match the greater thirst of the engine as it was developed.

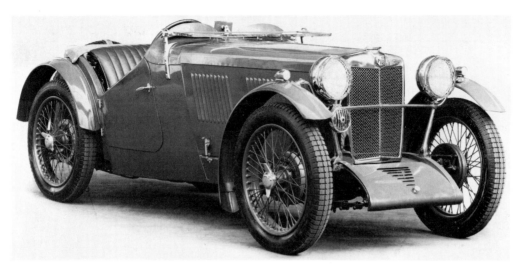

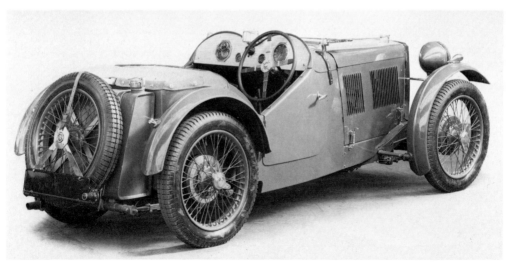

The highly popular J-type open two-seater, about the body of which *The Autocar* made the apposite comment: 'The whole car is essentially fitting for its intended work; its appearance alone is sufficient for most enthusiasts, appearance being almost as important as performance'. Interesting J-type features include the stout tubular crossmember across the rear of the chassis, with the battery cradle just ahead of it, the crossflow cylinder-head based on that of the C-type, black-rimmed dashboard instruments including a combined speedometer/rev counter, the sprung-spoked steering wheel, and the option

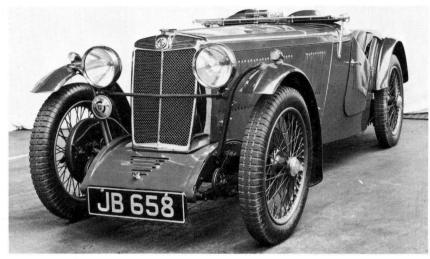

of headlamp stoneguards on the car pictured on the previous page which, in the lower picture, also displays bright-metal instrument surrounds. The J2 was priced competitively at £199 10s (£199.50). The larger 12-inch front brakes, however, pictured above, belong to the Magna F2 which, as the top picture confirms, shared the J2's body, although with the 1,271-cc six-cylinder engine.

The notorious 80-mph J2 supplied to *The Motor* for road test with a mildly tuned head. Unfortunately, the engine speed needed to achieve this speed was rather ambitious, and few privately owned J2 cranks could cope.

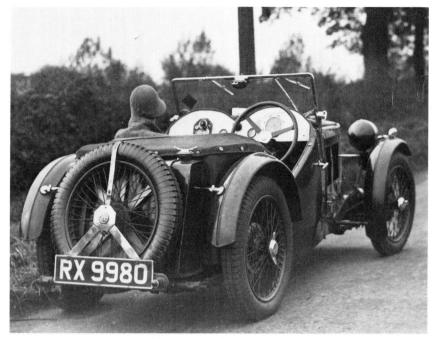

Thousands of J2 Midgets took to the hills in the early-1930s and here a private owner scatters the stones during an MGCC Abingdon trial. Note how car club badges have begun to proliferate.

The K1 four-seater tourer with bucket seats — a luxury denied occupants of the tiny Midget cockpit. The K1, with its 1,087-cc engine and preselector gearbox, tended to take over from the 18/80 Speed Model, and the development in four short years is striking, as these November 1932 pictures show. The K-type cars featured a split track rod mechanism, which improved handling, and although it had an elaborate body for a 40-bhp engine the car was no slouch.

The twin-carburettor layout of the standard J-type engine. Note that all the pipework is in rigid copper.

The blown J3 Midget, with its SU carburettor dashpot just visible protruding coyly through the dumbiron fairing.

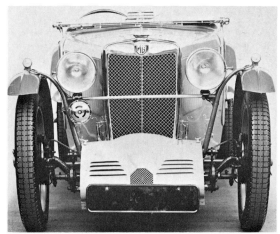

The front axle of the J3 coupled to a wide ribbed brake drum. The mounting of the wing stay is clearly visible in the foreground.

Installation of the Powerplus 6A blower in the J3 with the mounting pads for the radiator visible behind the crossmember. Only one induction pipe was now supplied, suggesting that the low-speed running problems were past, or that MG no longer considered blown types as serious road cars.

More J3 engine detail revealing the high quality of the engineering. The ancestry is clearly evident, with features of the Minor engine from which it was descended still on display.

The J3 served on many a campaign, and in the 1936 Paris-St Raphael rally — an all-ladies event — Comtesse Moy did well with her fully equipped example, winning the 1,100-cc class of the hill-climb with her 750-cc car and finishing ninth in classification.

A radiator mascot, headlamp stoneguards, badge bar, spotlamps and bumpers, as well as tinted glass, have been added to this late version of a Mark II saloon, the last of which left Abingdon in July 1933, though some remained unsold for a year or more. By then the car was being undercut by cosmetically more attractive cars.

The L-type Magna chassis, equipped with 1,086-cc engine, a pleasing crash gearbox and Marles-Weller steering. The K-type engine gave it ample performance, but roadholding was not up to K standards.

The KA-series engine with its 3 SU carburettors gave 39 bhp at 5,500 rpm. Once again there are no flexible pipes. The exhaust porting on these engines was most effective, but the inlet was less successful.

The K2 two-seater was offered at £390 with a 1,286-cc engine, the size being chosen to differentiate it from the Wolseley-based engine of the earlier F1.

The dash panel of the K2, which featured a Brooklands sprung-spoke steering wheel. The rev counter and speedometer are separate instruments, and as always the minor controls were neatly arranged close to the gearlever. Note that the gearbox housing is embossed with the MG octagon.

The timber-framed structure of a K-series saloon body can be seen clearly in this view of a unit awaiting its outer skins and trim.

The work of the French school of coachwork designers was much admired in Britain and Kimber had this Continental Coupe, with its nod in the direction of Jean Bugatti and his 'coaches', built for the L Magna chassis. It sold slowly at £350. Unfortunately, the sloping radiator of the Magna chassis did not marry well with the verticals of the body.

Horton passes a line of workmen keeping the track clear of stones as he collects a set of 750-cc class world records at over 111 mph for 100 miles, 200 kilometres and one hour in May 1934, at Brooklands.

The previous month, Horton had been down to Brooklands for an attempt on the 50 and 100 kilometres and one hour records with his very effective 750-cc record-breaker, which is seen above passing the timekeeper's box at the Fork. Below, when the Magic Midget was no longer required for record-breaking, Enever, seated in the car, updated it, giving it a 146-bhp Q-type engine and bigger brakes and sent it off to Germany with a road-racing body.

The 1933 Magna L1 four-seater, which featured the 1,087-cc engine in twin-carburettor form. Note how high the rear seat is placed relative to the bucket-type front seats.

The more rakish lines of the Magna L2 two-seater, the twin seats of which share a common backrest. The 'MG' badge is neatly mounted into the centre of the spare wheel securing straps.

The road-racing J4 Midget used a beguiling combination of production parts to provide roadholding and braking not quite in keeping with the potential of the highly developed blown 750-cc engine. The Powerplus blower gave up to 18 psi boost to give some 70-plus bhp at 6,000 rpm, and with a top speed in excess of 125 mph with the right gearing the shortcomings of the short-wheelbase J2 chassis became apparent. The car featured L2 12-inch brakes and a C-type gearbox.

The cockpit of the L2 Magna with the octagon theme displayed on instruments, steering wheel boss and gearlever housing.

The third K3 Magnette built, chassis 003. The K3 was the quintessence of the classic road-racing car. Not particularly light, but immensely powerful and strong, it was capable of maintaining its performance over long distances and represented a fascinating mixture of advanced engine technology and obsolete chassis design.

The very first K3, as driven by Wright in the 1933 Monte Carlo Rally. It survived into the late-1930s in its original form and is seen here in a Bugatti Owners Club Amersham hill-climb. The very deep scuttle cowls and high-mounted spare wheel can be seen clearly. In the days before Prescott the BOC had to stage their events on loose-surfaced hills.

This was the second prototype K3, which was used as a training car for the 1933 Mille Miglia. Liberal use of mesh has been made for front-end protection, and a rather unattractive cowl has been added hurriedly.

The MG team pose at Brescia before the start of the 1933 Mille Miglia. From left to right can be seen Hamilton, Earl Howe, Ferrari, Count Lurani, Eyston, Marchese Pariso, Birkin, Rubin and McConnell.

Gordon Crosby's painting of Nuvolari passing the J4 of Hamilton as it makes its disastrous pit stop in the closing stages of the 1933 TT race.

A superb study of the purposeful 1934 K3. Offered as a road-racer, with just a nod in the direction of road use, the car cost £795. Despite the bluff radiator, the frontal area was quite modest and the general outline was clean. A Roots-type Marshall was now the preferred blower.

The delivery bay at Abingdon. Jackson is sitting in the blown J4, while Kohlrausch's mechanic is in a K3 similar to the TT winner of 1933. Amongst the Magnettes awaiting delivery, behind, is 'Old No 1' with its vee screen.

The MG Zoller Special, which Eddie Hall developed for hill-climbing in 1935. Here it is at Shelsley Walsh as Hall accelerates through the Esses. To lighten the car the rear body section was made of canvas.

Hefty drum brakes and 4.75−19 tyres were standard equipment for K-series cars.

The 1,271-cc N and KN engine with its widely spaced twin SU carburettors fed from SU electric pumps through flexible delivery pipes.

A line-up of engines awaiting installation into K-type chassis in one part of the Abingdon assembly area, above. The front view of this 1934 K3, below, points up the family resemblance with MG's more mundane products. The brakes have twin-lever operation and are protected by wire-mesh airscoops. In the background, a production MG chassis awaits its bodywork.

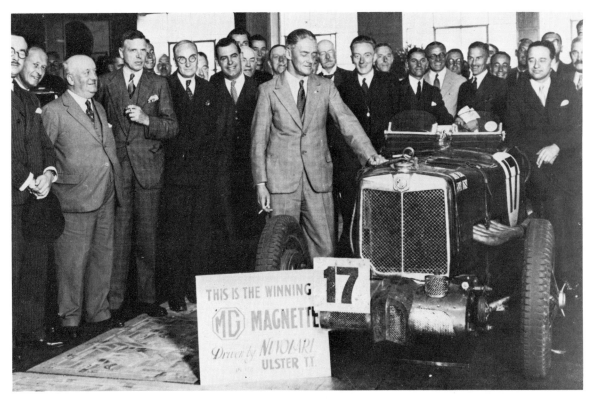

Sir William Morris and colleagues proudly displaying Nuvolari's 1933 Ulster TT-winning K3 Magnette after its return to Oxford. Below, although few K3s escaped modification, this original-looking example was seen competing against a T-series Midget in a Continental road race many years after its heyday.

An early picture of a PA Midget two-seater, above, revealing recessed trafficators as a concession to MG's widening public. The rear three-quarters view, below, shows that the style gradually developed during the early-1930s has been nearly refined for the new model. The delicacy of the swept wings was something which even the later T-types could not emulate fully.

The P-type chassis, revealing clearly the line of the propeller-shaft with the remote-control mechanism for the gearbox above it, and the transverse location of the batteries behind the rear axle.

A PB dashboard, with a large-diameter rev-counter immediately ahead of the driver and a smaller speedometer in the centre of the panel.

The quick-release fuel filler cap on a PB has a quality of finish which would not disgrace a car costing two or three times as much.

The P-type four-seater, although a pretty car, was another MG tourer with steering problems when all four seats were occupied by adult passengers.

Two views of the PB, which was introduced with a 939-cc engine offering 44 bhp in order to meet the challenge from larger-engined cars from other manufacturers. The 847-cc PA had become significantly underpowered.

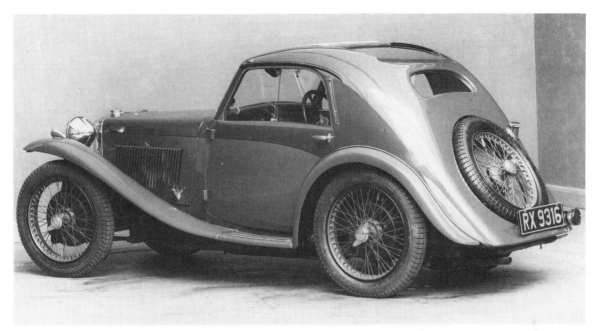

The Airline body, above, was an interesting departure for MG and provided further evidence of the widening of the market for the Midget range. Note that the doors are front-hinged and have sliding windows, while the location of trafficators just forward of the rear end of the drip channels is a particularly neat installation. The aerodynamic efficiency of this model, however, was probably not as favourable as might have appeared, the front end of the car being virtually unaltered from standard. The Midget had inherited a vertically slatted radiator by the time of the introduction of the PB, below, although the basic profile of the PA remained in evidence.

One of the 1936 Cream Crackers, JB 7525 is seen here in its natural habitat. This Marshall-supercharged PB was one of the team of three which, although privately owned, were sponsored by the factory. With drivers of the calibre of Toulmin, Bostock and Macdermid, they were the team to beat on the trials hills from 1936 onwards.

The Navy gives the once-over to George Eyston's Dancing Daughters on a quayside. The 847-cc PA Midgets, driven by all-women crews at Le Mans in 1935, were competently handled and ran reliably through the 24 hours, although they were outpaced in their class by the larger Singers.

In place of the C-type, which had proved such a handful, the Q-type Midget was introduced in 1934 and was sold as an outright racer with a body conforming to AIACR regulations.

Noble in his single-seater Midget lines up with a brace of Austin Sevens for the start of the 1937 500 Miles race at Brooklands. This car eventually succeeded in lapping the outer circuit at over 122 mph, which says volumes for both the skill and courage of the driver.

The Zoller blower installation on the 750-cc Q-type racing engine. The vane-type unit was evolved by McEvoy and gave 25 psi pressure. It was driven from the front of the crankshaft through a universal and a reduction gear.

111

The KN pillarless saloon, by now fitted with a more powerful 56-bhp engine, was an elaborate and well fitted-up car, but was possibly rather expensive for those difficult days.

The interior of the KN, showing its comprehensive instrumentation and the generously proportioned pneumatic seat cushions, which offered a considerable degree of comfort. The body was built on a flexibly mounted subframe.

Sliding windows, pillarless door construction and somewhat claustrophobic rear quarters were features of the KN, the interior design of which presented a curious mixture of curved lines.

George Eyston in the R-type before the car's debut in the 1935 International Trophy race at Brooklands, where, despite teething problems, two cars finished the course. Further development of the cars was halted by Nuffield's ban on MG's racing activities, but private owners carried on the work, even evolving a twin-overhead-camshaft head.

This picture of one of the 1935 team cars in the Mannin Beg illustrates clearly why the drivers of the period were inclined to distrust wheels which performed antics like this R-type, seen turning right at the traffic lights. The team cars all retired from this event.

The introduction of the works racing R-type 750-cc single-seater in 1935 marked the dawning of a new era at Abingdon. Here at last was a chassis to the same standards of scientific achievement as had been applied to the engines. The general scheme, with a backbone chassis, fully independent wishbone suspension and a highly stressed powerplant, was full of potential.

Concern to pare away unsprung weight and a desire to ensure controlled location of the wheel movement is evident. The only misjudgment is in the use of equal-length wishbones, which led to the lean problems due to parallelogramming illustrated on the previous page. The results of research into suspension by the General Motors team under Olley had yet to be published.

After the R-types had been sold-off following the decision by Nuffield to give up racing, Evans, believing that much more power would be available from a twin-overhead-camshaft head, commissioned one from McEvoy. The large downdraught SU carburettor is fed through oversize pipes from a double fuel pump, while Allen screws secure the water header pipes to the head.

The backbone frame of the R-type weighed just 57 lb. It was the work of Frank Stevens, who had been responsible for the chassis of the Kimber Special 10 years earlier.

One of the Zoller-blown 750-cc racing engines on test. Work was still being carried out at Abingdon on high-performance projects, either for customers, or for the company's future projects.

Meanwhile, production of the much less advanced Abingdon models continued, and here is an example of the NA Magnette with the hood up, showing the generous window area provided for rear-seat passengers who, inevitably, were rather cramped due to the limitations of an 8-ft wheelbase chassis.

The NA in two-seater form, the lines of which, though less graceful than those of the Midget, were aided by the two-tone colour scheme. With its 1,271-cc, 56.6-bhp engine and a top speed of over 80 mph, the NA was a brisk performer. Note the additional rev-counter below the dashboard.

Although the NA range was not particularly cheap — this model sold for £335 — the cars were given an excellent finish and were generally well equipped.

Although the front-seat passengers of the NA were well protected, at anything above 40 mph the rear-seat occupants were severely weather-buffeted by the slipstream and their location aft of the rear axle was less than ideal.

The NA was quite a striking car on the road, and the badge bar at the front was a desirable addition for the insignia-conscious club motorist of the time.

Beneath the dashboard, the floor area was strictly functional and little attempt was made to deaden the noise from the engine and transmission. As a result, the cars were particularly noisy to ride in with the hood up.

The NB Magnette was a more refined version of its predecessor. Doors were now front-hinged, the radiator had vertical slats and substantial upholstering was provided for the one-piece seat backrest.

A chrome flash was introduced to carry the eye past the awkward line below the windscreen and the door hinges were lengthened and streamlined to accentuate, in the upper case, the break line of the two-tone colour scheme.

The cumbersome hood frame of the four-seater NB tended to mar the lines of this model at the rear, which lacked the grace of its two-seater counterpart.

Back to the track and the sight of an unblown NE Magnette being passed by the low-chassis Lagonda of Field. The mandatory Brooklands bonnet strap is a reminder of the origin of what became one of the most overworked symbols of the prewar sports car.

Rationalization was the Morris Motors slogan through the 1930s, and one effect of this was that MG left coachbuilders such as Carbodies and went to the Morris body shops, where elaborate facilities were available for the examination of mock-ups before they were given approval for production. This is a fully panelled mock-up for the 2-Litre saloon, which took MG into a new market in 1936. The bolt-on wheels were to be discarded in favour of the centre-lock variety, and the clumsy rear bumper was also replaced.

The rear compartment of the same mock-up showing the wide expanse of sliding roof and the deep foot wells. Once again MG plumped for a chassis with a semi-cruciform to permit adequate rear-seat leg space.

No doubt at all that this is also a mock-up, or why second thoughts had to be given to the gearbox installation. Octagonal instrument surrounds have departed for the time being, but the theme is still carried on with the pedal rubbers and the window winders.

Midget and six-cylinder production running side-by-side at Abingdon. An overhead conveyor is used to transport wheels, but the cars are still pushed from station to station by hand.

The 2-Litre saloon was harmonious from any angle. The twin pass lamps were arranged to act as dipped headlamps. The built-in hydraulic jacks can be seen protruding beneath the car.

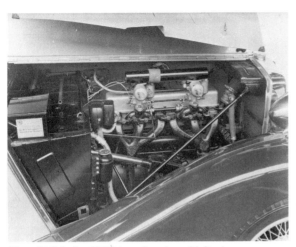 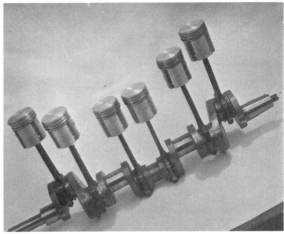

The tall Wolseley 18/80-based engine with its deep sump presented Abingdon with considerable installation problems, and the solution for the MG 2-Litre was to use downdraught SU carburettors with horizontal dashpots to enable the bonnet line to be kept low. The right-hand picture shows the crankshaft and piston assemblies of the 2,288-cc engine, the basic design of which had been well proven in Morris and Wolseley models from the Nuffield stable.

Kimber had a liking for taut-looking sports tourers, and this superb four-seater on the 2-Litre chassis must have been much to his taste. It was one of a short series built by Charlesworth, a coachbuilder with a considerable reputation for Alvis derivatives.

The 2-Litre chassis was provided for Salmons, the coachbuilding company which was eventually to become part of Aston Martin Lagonda, who produced this most attractive Tickford four-seater drophead body with a three-position hood, the intermediate sedanca de ville position providing rear passengers with sheltered accommodation with plenty of fresh air. The keen eye will detect subtle differences between these two prototypes, including a variation in windscreen height. Below, the robust 2-Litre chassis, the engine displacement of which was increased from its initial 2,288 cc to 2,322 cc as a result of a small increase in cylinder bore several months after the car was put into production.

The 2-Litre SA Tickford drophead coupe in open form looked a little untidy around the area of the hood irons, but was nevertheless an elegant looking car overall. Note the wooden door cappings and the elasticated pockets in the back of the front seats.

Notwithstanding Morris' pressed-steel expertize, MG's touring cars were still being assembled from handworked panels and wooden frames.

A new Midget. This is the T-type chassis, forerunner of a car which was to pave the way for MG's great export success. The line of descent from the C-type is evident, although the size had continued to increase, the wheelbase now being 7 ft 10 in and the track 3 ft 9 in.

This side view of a jacked-up TA chassis shows clearly the pressed-steel scuttle, an important innovation which served to insulate occupants from the noise and fumes from the engine, while retaining the traditional long bonnet of the Midget.

This overhead shot emphasizes the broad similarity of the T-type body shape with that of the PB which it replaced, although the newer car has a slightly more upright stance.

The rear view was as cobby as ever and the overall impression was one of great neatness. The fuel filler had been moved across to the left side of the slab-type tank.

Hood-up on the T-type, the well fitting software providing the most snug of Midgets produced so far. As with previous models, a fold-flat windscreen is a feature.

The instrument layout of the production TA Midget, with the speedometer moved over to the passenger's side of the cockpit and the rev-counter immediately ahead of the driver and incorporating a small clock in its dial. More generous carpeting and interior body trim is evident than on previous Midgets.

There were subtle changes from the final specification on the T-type which was prepared for the new Midget's Motor Show debut in London, including the location of the dashboard illumination.

Based on the current overhead-valve Wolseley Ten engine, the TA's MPJG four-cylinder power unit, at 1,292 cc, was a little larger than the earlier 'six' used in the Magnette. Cylinder dimensions of 63.5 x 102 mm made it a tall, narrow and compact engine, which fitted neatly into the Midget body. The main source of complaint was to be its limited tuning potential with both carburettors and exhaust located on the same side of the head.

Designed originally for a well-equipped, medium-priced saloon, the TA's MPJA engine was mounted on rubber and was equipped with a breather which fed the rocker cover fumes into the carburettors and a crankcase breather which carried fumes well away below the car. The dynamo was now belt-driven.

The TA's cork disc-lined clutch ran in oil and was very sweet to use, although somewhat soft in action.

The T-type MG Midget looks a most impressive sports car from this angle. The number on the plate, of course, is a fake and refers to the model designation and the fact that it was introduced at a price of £222 on the UK market.

The Lockheed hydraulic brakes offered on the TA, with 9-inch drums, were smaller but wider than the brakes on the PB and offered not only improved braking performance and greater durability but also simpler servicing.

Two views of the original T-type Midget with the hood erect, the car at this stage still lacking the trafficators fitted to production models. Twin rear panels in the hood gave barely tolerable rearward visibility, but were typical of the period, and at least the driver had the benefit of a scuttle-mounted exterior mirror. The 'MG' badge is recessed into the hub cap of the spare wheel, but not of the road wheels.

The soon-to-be-famous XPAG engine, based on that used for the Morris Ten saloon, made its debut in the T-type MG with the announcement of the TB version in 1939. Although the MG's capacity had gone down from 1,292 cc to 1,250 cc, performance and tuning potential had both been improved.

The bottom end of the XPAG engine showing its three-bearing crankshaft, the shell bearings and their caps.

The four-branch exhaust manifold nestling below the twin SU carburettors of the XPAG engine, which produced over 54 bhp at 5,000 rpm in this form.

This luggage grid was offered by the factory as an extra for the TB Midget. The car can be recognized as such, rather than as a TC, because the spokes do not extend beyond the centre of the wheels.

One of the TA Cream Cracker trials cars. The engine was a 1,548-cc unit from the VA range, later bored out to 1,708 cc. The front tyres are standard-size knobblies, the driving wheels have ordinary tyres, and the spares are oversize knobblies on an extended carrier.

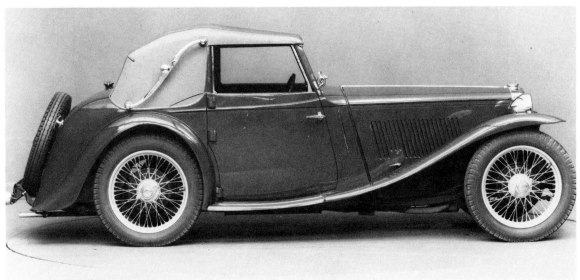

The prototype TA drophead was either deemed too costly to build to the £270 price limit set for it, or was considered to look too heavy around the rear quarters.

The production T-type drophead, another Tickford design, was well equipped. The slightly wider body enabled bucket seats to be accommodated and the steering column was adjustable vertically as well as fore-and-aft. Performance was slightly down on the open two-seater due to the extra weight.

Two teams of TAs were produced for the 1937 competitions season, and here is Toulmin tackling Dancers Hill in BBL 78, one of the Cream Crackers cars distinguished by a chocolate-and-cream colour scheme.

The other team were known as the Three Musketeers, and here is Bostock in one of the red-painted cars working hard to maintain momentum after a sharp right-hand turn on muddy ground. These TAs were to be blown for the 1938-39 trials season.

The 1½-litre four-cylinder VA engine was based on the unit used in the Wolseley 12/48 and Morris 12 Series 3 models. It offered 54 bhp from a displacement of 1,548 cc.

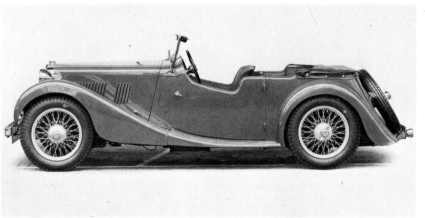

One of three models offered in the VA series, this four-seater open tourer was produced for MG by Charlesworth and offered a characteristic simplicity of line and a commendable overall neatness. Marketed as the 1½-Litre, the range also included a four-door saloon and a four-seater drophead coupe.

The 1½-Litre in rolling chassis form. Visible in the foreground are the torque reaction rod for the front axle and one of the built-in Jackall jacks.

The VA chassis was a substantial affair, the longitudinal members being overswept at the rear. The channel sections were boxed and stout tubular members provided the cross-bracing. The stabilizer bumper was fitted to damp out torsional flexing at the front-end.

The cockpit of the open-tourer version of the VA 1½-Litre showing the instruments contained within four circular dials, the outer pair being divided into two segments. The fold-flat windscreen continued the design theme established with earlier and more sporting open models.

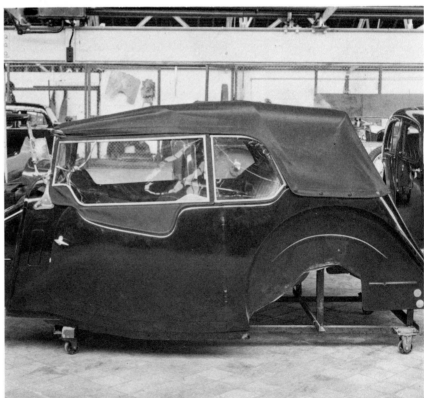

A basically similar dashboard layout was integrated into the more substantial coachwork of the VA saloon, and in this example an optional radio has been added beneath the main control panel. The organ-type accelerator pedal became an increasingly popular fitment in the late-1930s.

138

A trolley-mounted body for the 1½-Litre open tourer, fully trimmed and with hood and sidescreens fitting well, awaiting delivery to its chassis.

The four-light saloon version of the VA was the most popular model in the range and bore more than a passing resemblance to the contemporary and rival Jaguar 1½-Litre saloon. The side-mounted spare wheel relieves what might otherwise have been a rather heavy side appearance.

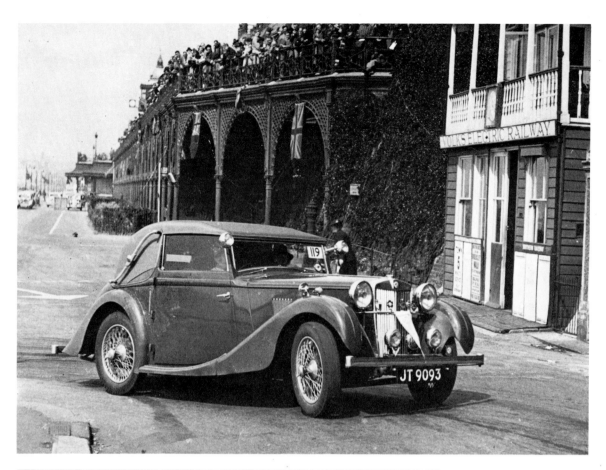

The Tickford-bodied drophead coupe version of the VA 1½-Litre, in this instance taking part in the 1939 RAC Brighton Rally. The screen pillar-mounted auxiliary lights, of course, were extras, as were the wing mirrors.

Final inspection and adjustments for lines of four-cylinder and six-cylinder saloons at Abingdon before the cars are sent on their way. The larger cars have twin horns and a spotlamp mounted centrally on a bar at the front, but the VA has to suffice with a single horn.

Which ever way you looked at it, the 2.6-Litre WA saloon was a handsome car. The upper picture shows a production model with a scuttle ventilator visible as a reminder that this model was notable for its foot-frying capabilities. The lower picture must have been of an earlier example before the ventilators had been added. The divided rear window is of generous size, and necessarily so for such a long car. Seen from the front, the WA is an excellent example of the dignity of style achieved by the better car manufacturers during the years immediately prior to the Second World War.

The rear compartment of a Tickford-bodied drophead coupe on the 2.6-Litre WA chassis showing a separate seat cushion for each of the rear passengers, and tipping front seats to ease access.

Octagonal instruments are back for the dashboard of the six-cylinder MGs and the theme is carried on for the steering wheel hub cover. The remote-control gearlever is conveniently placed relative to the steering wheel.

Two-colour instrument dials have been provided for this drophead version of the six-cylinder MG which, like the saloon, has an opening windscreen as an aid to further ventilation. Note the different location for the door window winder.

This magnificent fitted tool tray in the bootlid of a WA saloon is in marked contrast with the very rudimentary tools usually supplied with cars of this class some 40 or more years later.

Although by no means large by present-day standards, the luggage accommodation of the WA was reasonable for the time, and with care there was always the possibility of supporting extra luggage on the lowered lid, thanks to its two well anchored support straps.

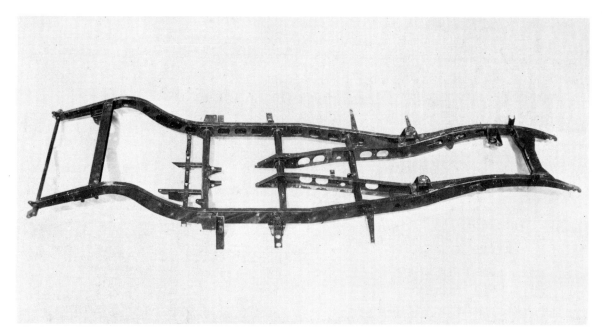

The chassis of the WA resembled closely that of the earlier 2-Litre model, although it had to accommodate a rear axle some 3 3/8 inches wider.

The six-cylinder engine in its 2.6-litre form with its twin SU carburettors drawing air through twin air cleaners linked to a common air silencer manifold.

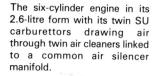

The robust crankshaft of the 2.6-litre engine, which produced over 95 bhp at 4,400 rpm as fitted to the WA models.

Still keen to encourage owners to lubricate their cars, Kimber insisted on grouped nipples and on the 2.6-Litre he placed them as conveniently as possible. Note that twin SU fuel pumps were provided to cope with the car's considerable thirst, and that the wipers were recessed neatly when parked.

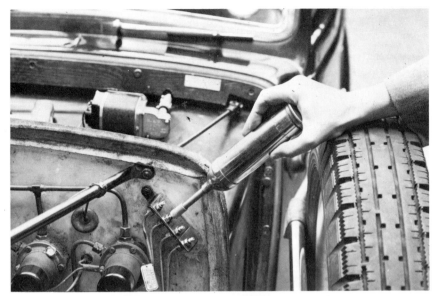

This spring-loaded device clamped to the front springs of the 2.6-Litre was intended to assist the spring shackle to damp out the kickback from road wheel shocks.

A rolling chassis for the 2.6-Litre, showing the generously proportioned rear footwells provided between the cross-bracing members and emphasizing the length of the steering column and the considerable distance between steering wheel and engine bulkhead.

Although EX 135 gained most fame as Goldie Gardner's record-breaker, it began life late in 1933 in this form, above, for Eyston to use as a record-breaker and with alternative bodywork for road-racing. With distinctive 'humbug' paintwork, the Magic Magnette gave Eyston the 1,100-cc flying-mile and kilometre records at over 128 mph and the one-hour record at 120.9 mph in October 1934. Goldie Gardner is seen below, in 1937, with the ex-Horton K3 Magnette record-breaker, which was to collect records at over 148 mph on a Frankfurt autobahn later in the year. In due course its engine was to find its way into EX 135.

With Goldie Gardner in the cockpit and Lord Nuffield standing alongside, EX 135 is unveiled with its new Reid Railton-designed body, based on German aerodynamics practice, in July 1938. Initially, the car was finished in silver green.

Enever and Cousins turn EX 135 round after a run in the 1938 series on the Frankfurt-Heidelburg autobahn, where the car averaged 187.6 mph over the flying-mile, to set a new 1,100-cc class record at figures higher than the current 1,500-cc and 3,000-cc class records. The extension to the air intake had been fabricated because during earlier runs misfiring had suggested airflow problems in the intake area.

147

By now in darker green livery and with the air intake flush-fitting, the Gardner MG returned to Germany and the Dessau autobahn in June 1939. On test, the engine had given 202 bhp at 7,500 rpm, and after a warming-up run the car recorded 203.9 mph over the flying-mile, setting a 1,100-cc class record that was to remain unbroken. After boring-out the engine with a portable jig borer to bring it into the next class, further runs were made and 1,500-cc records were set at 200.6 mph for five kilometres and 204.2 mph for the flying-mile.

Gardner and Enever examining the top-end of the engine being prepared for the 1939 runs.

The small-bore 750-cc block, blower rotor and blower casing with its twin SU carburettors which had been assembled in 1939 for EX 135 to tackle some further class records, before war put an end to all record-breaking activities for several years.

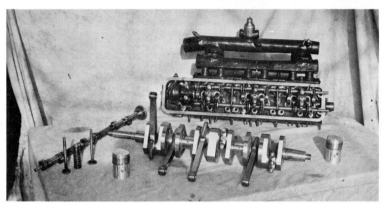

More EX 135 engine detail, in this case the cylinder-head with inlet manifold, crankshaft, connecting rods, pistons, camshaft, valves and a valve spring.

A signed photograph of Goldie Gardner, complete with characteristic pipe and walking stick, and with EX 135 still bearing evidence of minor battle scars from its prewar record-breaking activities.

The Morris Motors management had their own ideas about the kind of MG they ought to be building next, and their thoughts centred on the Morris Eight Series E which, unlike the Ten Series M, still retained a separate chassis. This mock-up, using suitably adapted Eight panels, was erected at Cowley early in 1939.

The rear view of the same MG Ten mock-up, showing the break line where the MG boot was grafted on to the Morris panels. At this stage the car's wheels have a distinct Wolseley flavour. After the war, of course, the small MG saloon would be introduced as the 1 ¼ -Litre.

The simplified interior of the prototype with a long cranked gearlever having considerable knuckle-scarring possibilities. The instrumentation is strongly Morris, although the adjustable steering column has the familiar MG look.

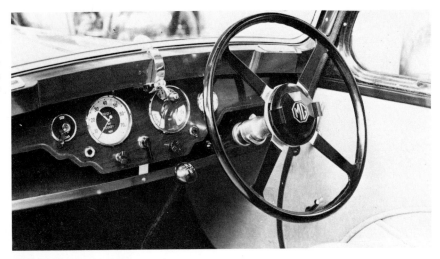

Issigonis and Daniels devised a system of independent front suspension using unequal-length wishbones and coil springs, together with rack-and-pinion steering, using the rigid hull of the Ten Series M as a base, but the layout remained on ice until it was applied to the postwar MG 1¼-Litre saloon.

The Y-type chassis of the 1¼-Litre saloon, with boxed main members. The absence of a front axle beam meant that the engine could be mounted well forward. Note the different cranked gearlever and the conveniently located handbrake.

One of the most appealing pictures of any MG archive, this photograph of an early postwar TC Midget was taken in the appropriately peaceful environment of the meadows near the Berkshire village of Long Wittenham.

The same car with the screen erect, confirming that the TC was virtually identical to the short-lived TB apart from minor but useful dimensional changes.

Mechanical changes introduced with the TC included a new voltage regulator, while rubber mountings were now provided at the front of the engine, and the battery was repositioned in a locker in the engine compartment.

A picture which accentuates the accessibility of the TC engine and its components and reveals the 'MG' octagon once again, this time on the oil dipstick. Note also the different air cleaner layout.

The XPAG engine, clutch and gearbox assembly, complete with remote-control lever. Note the substantial ribbing of the deep sump.

Low-pressure blowers such as the Marshall unit had a following in the early-postwar era as a method of instantly increasing the power of the XPAG engine. Using a compression ratio of around 8.5:1 the engine could handle pressure up to 4 psi.

Not even the most dedicated MG enthusiast could claim that the TC chassis had one of the world's great front ends. The skinny road springs, slender dumbirons and the lack of any stiffening from engine or body ensured that front axle control was always on the vague side.

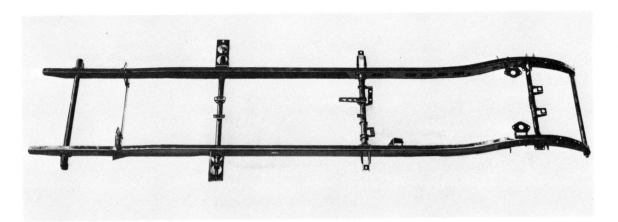

A picture which says it all. The slenderness of a bare TC chassis is unmistakable.

The location of a single 12-volt battery on the scuttle identifies this Midget chassis as a TC. Rear spring shackles with rubber bushes have replaced the former sliding trunnions used on earlier Midgets.

The TC was made 3 inches wider than the TB and the squab was deepened slightly by the use of the prewar TB drophead coupe body frame.

The TC Midget in side elevation — the classic lines of a sports car which was to do much to relieve the austerity of the early-postwar motoring world.

The definitive front view of a later TC. The modest brake drums look dwarfed within the 19-inch road wheels.

Headlamp beam adjustment in the Abingdon service bay. Headlamp support arms were bolted between the radiator surround and front wings on the TC.

The view which most TC drivers liked to display to other road users, but with twin shallow rear windows their own view of the road behind was relatively restricted.

157

The immediate postwar MG range, consisting of the Midget, revamped as the TC, and what might otherwise have been the MG Ten, but in fact became known as the 1¼-Litre. The saloon was 5 inches longer in the wheelbase and 5 inches wider than the two-seater.

Although bumpers were considered superfluous on the Midget for the UK market, MG's export aspirations meant that provision had to be made for them and they became familiar wear in some overseas markets.

158

An interesting overhead view of a TC chassis showing clearly the cable and pipe runs for the various services. The air cleaner seems to have found an unusual home in the scuttle, however.

A TC chassis hoisted for a final check. There is a legend that as these chassis came off the line they were approached by a burly character who, if all did not rotate as it should, gave one end of a dumbiron a resounding clout, whereupon everything would click into place. If that were so, this is where it would have happened . . .

TC Midgets and Y-type saloons take shape on parallel lines in the Abingdon assembly area.

By 1950 it was time to update the TC. Abingdon had their own plans, but several outsiders had their own ideas. Harry Lester built a series of very attractive tubular-framed MG specials for the currently popular airfield racing. Weighing some 10½ cwt, the car featured Y-type front suspension and a 4.9:1 final-drive ratio. The engine was linered down to 1,100 cc and 60 bhp was spoken of with a compression ratio of 9.2:1.

Despite its shortcomings, the TC was probably raced more frequently than any other sports car of its time. Here is a stripped example taking part in a Leinster road race.

161

The independent front suspension of the Y-type 1¼-Litre saloon featuring unequal-length wishbones and coil springs and with the steering rack mounted ahead of the suspension units.

The single-carburettor version of the trusty XPAG engine was adopted as the power unit for the 1¼-Litre saloon, in which form it produced 46 bhp at 4,800 rpm.

As in the TC, the 12-volt battery lived close above the engine, in a box on the bulkhead. All the electrical components were confined to one side of the engine, with the carburation and exhaust system on the other. The built-in jack and its pump are prominent.

Although it looked long and willowy, the gearchange on the Y-type saloon was quite acceptable. The steering wheel was adjustable for height and reach, the screen opened, as did the roof, and the seats were adequate for four good-size adults. The only real complaint was that the car was just too heavy.

The Y-type saloon as seen from the front, with the built-in jacks protruding beneath the body and a single auxiliary lamp mounted inboard of the left wing. Once again, MG had achieved a splendid amalgam of dignity and elegance.

There was an air of quality about the dashboard area, the instruments, once again adopting the octagon theme, being a considerable improvement on those of the prototype MG Ten of 1939.

The sliding roof of the Y-type saloon, a standard feature befitting a high-quality car. The centre armrest of the rear seat can just be seen through the front passenger window.

The Y-type assembly line at Abingdon with an engine being lowered on to a chassis in the foreground.

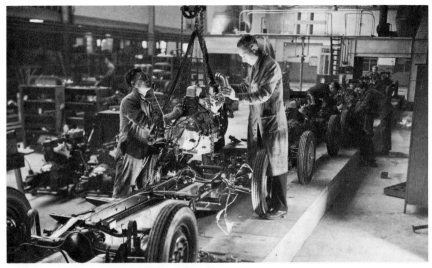

Moving on to the final assembly area, the main body section is suspended over a rolling chassis as a line of Y-type saloons near completion.

Body and bumpers are on, and now comes the first of the front wings, prior to the assembly of which the radiator cowl protection has been removed.

The detachable jack handle has been inserted into the jack pump of a Y-type, this worthwhile aid in the days of relatively frequent punctures being a carry-over from prewar MG saloon models.

A neat and compact car, with its lively 1,250-cc, 46-bhp engine and independent front suspension, the Y-type saloon was sufficiently ahead of many of its contemporaries to justify its premium price and was a popular choice of the impoverished-feeling middle classes in the late-1940s.

The YT was the open four-seater tourer version of the Y-type and was intended as an export-only car. Unfortunately, not everyone appreciated overseas that just because it was larger than the TC two-seater it must be assumed to be faster. This, of course, was definitely not the case, even though it shared the TC's twin-carburettor-equipped XPAG engine. A small number of YTs eventually found their way on to the UK market, and the car above is one of the right-hand-drive examples.

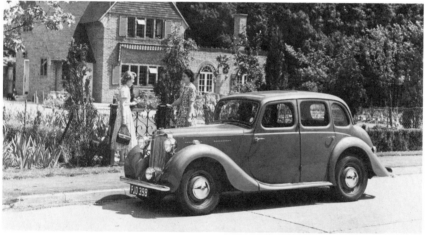

A reminder that screen demisting in cars was not always as efficient as we have become used to today. Here is a Y-type saloon with a pair of stick-on demisters of the type which were in widespread use at the time.

The original Y-type saloon became known retrospectively as the YA when an improved-specification version, with slightly smaller wheels and various minor mechanical refinements, was introduced in 1948 as the YB.

Italian coachwork design had yet to reach the heights it was to command in the late-1950s when Zagato, who never seemed at his best when using British chassis, produced this rather curious four-seater on the Y-type chassis.

Nuffield were not completely inactive in thought concerning passenger car projects during the war years, and Issigonis' Mosquito concept, which eventually was to emerge as the Morris Minor, was the most significant of them all. It was, perhaps, inevitable that the stylists at Cowley should consider an open two-seater derivative of this design and to contemplate it as a future MG Midget. Here are two views of a mock-up which depicted their ideas in 1947.

The mock-up was around for several years, and by 1948 it had inherited a hardtop. Other changes visible here are to the wheels, the use of smaller headlamps, subtle changes to the grille and different use of chrome along the centreline of the bonnet.

Once the final shape of the Morris Minor had been established, Cowley's badge engineers got to work on a possible MG version. The upper example at least had the merit of offering a tolerable compromise between the rounded lines of the Minor and the traditional vertical theme of the classic MG radiator. The alternative shown below, however, might have best been left unphotographed, unless it was needed as evidence of what not to do. Interestingly, the mock-up car was given a sliding roof, something from which the Minor might well have benefitted.

The project for a Midget Major did not progress far beyond this quarter-scale model. A pity, because the design had considerable merit.

Another proposal for an alternative MG front end for grafting on to the Minor shell, this time with the headlamps mounted much closer together.

The uncompromising MG radiator seen on the Minor mock-up on the left was also applied, along with a more substantial front bumper, to the Morris Oxford/Six shell, but in the end it was decided to confine such cars to the Morris and Wolseley ranges.

The first genuine postwar design for an MG two-seater appeared towards the end of 1949 as the TD. Although it retained the TC's wheelbase of 7 ft 10 in, the car had the wider tracks of the Y-type, as well as that car's independent front suspension. Gone, too, were the traditional MG wire-spoke wheels, at least for the present.

An early example of a TD, still without the ventilation holes on the road wheels, revealing the benefit of 20 years of experience in sports car manufacture in the production of a snug-fitting and weatherproof hood and sidescreens.

The front screen was still of the fold-flat variety and the traditional MG radiator shell was retained, but the latest Midget had bumpers front and rear and substantial overriders were a much needed addition for export markets in particular.

The independent front suspension of the TD was the result of research work carried out by Morris engineers in the late-1930s. In due course a TD Mark II was marketed, intended initially for competition work, which featured additional damping.

With the screen folded the TD has an eager air befitting a car which was destined to record many achievements on the race track during its relatively brief production life.

The cockpit of a left-hand-drive TD, showing the two main instrument dials immediately ahead of the driver and a lidded glove compartment in front of the passenger, with the control buttons and switches and minor instruments grouped in between.

A TD awaiting delivery, with a customer's car, complete with badge bar, badges and central spotlamp, behind and amongst a large quantity of RM-series Rileys, which were also assembled at Abingdon during the 1950s.

EX 135 reappeared after the war with a bubble-type cockpit canopy and Goldie Gardner was soon breaking records again. In October 1946 he broke the Magic Midget's 10-year-old speed for the flying-mile at 159.15 mph, then ran the car as a 500-cc by blanking off two of the six cylinders and recording 118.06 mph. In 1949, using a different engine in three-cylinder form, Gardner increased this speed for the mile to 154.23 mph, and finally, in 1950, the car ran as a twin-cylinder 350-cc and took the flying-mile record at 121.09 mph.

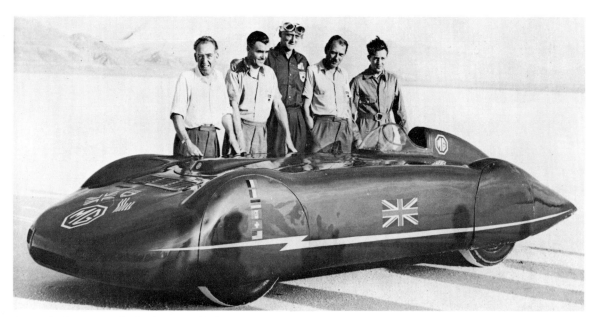

In search of more records, Gardner took EX 135 to the Bonneville Salt Flats in 1951, with a 1,250-cc XPAG engine installed giving 213 bhp with 30 psi of boost, but trouble with the timekeeping equipment caused the attempt to be abandoned. Here he is with his crew, including Enever and Jackson, on his return in 1952, the car carrying the insignia of the countries visited during its various sorties. EX 135 was also used for a crack at the 2-litre records, using a much modified Wolseley 6/80 engine of 2,215-cc, destroked to under the 2-litre limit. During the course of one of these runs Gardner spun off course and hit a marker post, which was flung against the cockpit canopy and knocked the driver on the head. Here he is, below, out of the car, somewhat dazed as a mechanic carries a wheel cover away from the scarred record-breaker. The following year, deteriorating health caused Gardner to abandon all further record attempts.

A record-breaker with the lid off. This is EX 135 with one of the XPAG engines installed and with the blower mounted ahead of the front-axle line and behind the water and oil radiators.

A transplant of a much-modified six-cylinder engine, based on the 2,215-cc Wolseley 6/80 power unit, enabled EX 135 to widen its record-breaking programme, although a series of misfortunes meant that the 1952 season brought considerably less success than had been anticipated.

The offset transmission line can be seen clearly in this rear view of EX 135 with the six-cylinder engine installed. With long-range fuel tanks strapped in place and a high-mounted instrument panel between them, the driver must have felt a little claustrophobic even before the body with its bubble canopy had been lowered around him.

This mock-up of the car which was to bring the Magnette name back into the MG catalogue lacked the grace of the final product, especially in the area of the radiator grille. The new car was to make use of the versatile 1,489-cc B-series engine at that time under development by the British Motor Corporation.

The one-piece rear-hinged lift-up bonnet was an unusual departure for MG, but it provided very reasonable engine-compartment access-ibility for the Magnette, although care had to be taken to avoid the sharp bottom corners of the radiator surround panel.

An early ZA Magnette in production form, revealing graceful lines which were also adopted for a contemporary Wolseley saloon, which was sold as the 4/44 with the 1,250-cc XPAG engine.

The dashboard area of the Magnette, with the MG octagon still present on the steering wheel boss, but only partly reproduced around the speedometer, which was flanked by four rectangular dials. Widespread use of walnut enhanced the quality image of the car.

The 1955 version of the ZA Magnette, with auxiliary lamps, improved wheel covers and benefitting aesthetically from the contrasting colour on the wheels.

With the ZA Magnette, MG had at last produced a full four-seater saloon of high quality and with full equipment which did not have to suffer the penalty of being grossly overweight.

The dashboard of the ZB version of the Magnette, which was produced between 1956 and 1959. The last of the ZA models had a similar interior layout except that the steering wheel was flat rather than dished and the ashtray was built into the top of the dashboard screen rail.

The ZB Magnette, mainly identifiable from a ZA by the larger rear screen and by the body-length chrome strips which provided the break line for the two colours of the Varitone version seen here. The Z-type Magnettes enjoyed some success in both rallying and saloon car racing.

The top end of the TD's 1,250-cc XPAG engine, which would be little changed until the availability of better-quality fuel enabled larger carburettors and valves and a higher compression ratio to be used, raising the power to 57 bhp at 5,500 rpm. On the right, a body is lowered carefully on to a TD chassis in the Abingdon assembly area.

George Phillips narrowly leading Ted Lund in their Mark II TDs during the Production Touring Car race at the BRDC's International Trophy meeting at Silverstone in 1950, when the three-car MG team, with Dick Jacobs in the other entry, finished behind Ruddock's 1,496-cc HRG in the 1½-litre class.

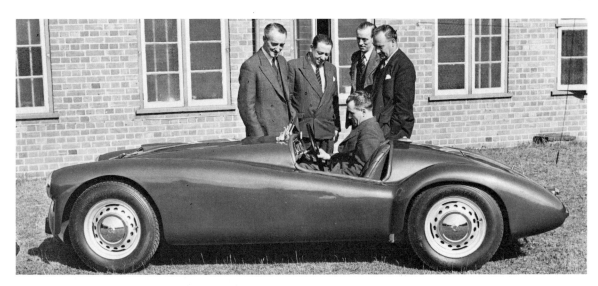

The TD which was built for Phillips to drive at Le Mans in 1951 and which had a body designed by Enever, who is seen here in the cockpit. Essentially the chassis was in standard race tune, although the rear-axle ratio was raised to give a top speed in excess of 115 mph. The car's run ended after three hours due to valve breakage.

The smoothly contoured lines of UMG 400 were to provide the inspiration for the body shape of the MGA, although the TF was due to appear first as an interim model. The cockpit of Phillips' Le Mans car had cut down body sides to provide sufficient elbow room for handling the large-diameter steering wheel.

An ingenious proposal by Nuffield designer Gerald Palmer for a successor to the TD Midget was that two cars should be offered, one with traditional and the other with more modern styling, but each based on the same chassis. Here are two views of his suggestion for the more traditional style, which incorporates swept wings and rear-hinged doors integrated into cut-down body sides.

The otherwise rather heavy side appearance of the more modern style is relieved by a long chrome flash above the wheelarches, while the body panels extend considerably below bumper height at both front and rear. In the event, the two-model plan was not adopted and MG enthusiasts were given the TF instead.

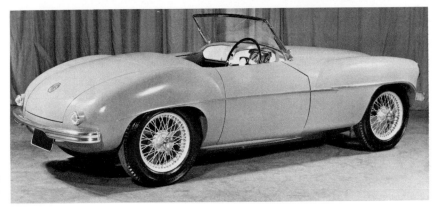

Although somewhat controversial at the time, with its retention of a classic shape but with concessions to more modern thinking, including semi-recessed headlamps and a sloping and curved radiator grille, the TF has subsequently achieved classic status and is a highly coveted Midget. This car has become part of the Leyland Historic Vehicles Collection.

The TF chassis, the radiator height of which was some 3½ inches lower than that of the TD, thereby allowing a lowering of the scuttle height as well. Although ventilated pressed-steel wheels were the standard fitment, wire-spoke wheels were a listed option.

The TF chassis in right-hand-drive form with the front suspension on considerable droop before being subjected to the weight of the bodywork. The high-mounted carburettor dashpots and the pancake-type air cleaners are a reminder that there was not much vertical clearance beneath the bonnet.

Destined for export, a left-hand-drive TF revealing quite an eager appearance from the front with its low-set headlamps recessed into wide front wing aprons.

The sloping spare wheel and wedge-shaped fuel tank are packaged neatly between the rear number plate and the optional luggage grid on this wire-wheeled TF.

Four more views of the TF, which began life as a 1,250-cc car but was destined to receive the larger-bore engine in due course, which increased its capacity to 1,466 cc. The retention of a centre-hinged two-piece bonnet considerably restricted access to the engine compartment. The lower picture on this page shows another example of a well-fitting MG hood which, as can be seen opposite, could be stowed neatly beneath its tonneau cover in the generous body space behind the seats. On the TF, the instruments had been moved back into the centre of the dashboard — a convenience when producing cars in both left-hand-drive and right-hand-drive form, as was the central handbrake — and the octagon had reappeared once more as a dashboard theme.

MG's record-breaking successor to EX 135, which was given the designation EX 179, undergoing tests on the banking at the Motor Industry Research Association test track near Nuneaton. Two versions of the 1,466-cc XPEG engine were used in this car, one for sprint runs and the other for endurance work.

The rolling chassis of EX 179, which was built up around the spare chassis-frame which had been constructed originally for EX 175, the prototype of what would become known as the MGA and which, in turn, had been inspired originally by the Phillips Le Mans car.

The cockpit area of EX 179, with the four-instrument dashboard ahead of a sprung steering wheel specially shaped to give adequate leg room in the straight-ahead position.

Ken Miles and George Eyston, who took the 10-mile record at 153.7 mph using the sprint engine in EX 179 and, with the endurance power unit, the six-hours record at 121.6 mph and the 12-hours at 120.87 mph.

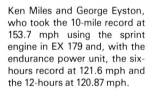

While EX 179 was busy collecting records, back at Abingdon Enever was busily engaged in thoughts about its successor. This model was used for preliminary tests of which would become EX 181.

The chassis of EX 175 became the prototype of the MGA and featured the well-tried wishbone-and-coil-spring front suspension from the TF and half-elliptic rear leaf springs.

Registered HMO 6, EX 175 differed only slightly in body detail from the production MGA, one of the items destined not to be adopted being the variable-rake windscreen.

The hood of the prototype car incorporated a plastic light in the roof, while the power bulge on the bonnet was only necessary because EX 175 was fitted with the taller TD-type XPAG engine, whereas the MGA would have the BMC B-series engine.

The dashboard of the production prototype MGA, with instruments sensibly back in front of the driver and the rev-counter having its orange sector starting at 5,500 rpm and the red sector at 6,000 rpm. The central horn button is surrounded by the loudspeaker for the radio.

White-wall tyres adorn the production prototype MGA, the hood of which has an unusually large rear screen panel by the standards of the day.

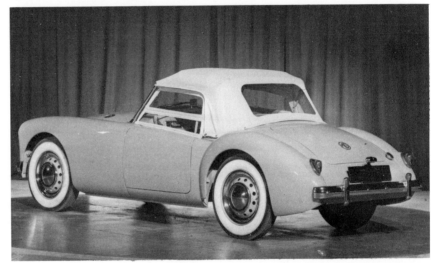

The slim bumper overriders on the prototype car were to be replaced by more substantial examples on production models.

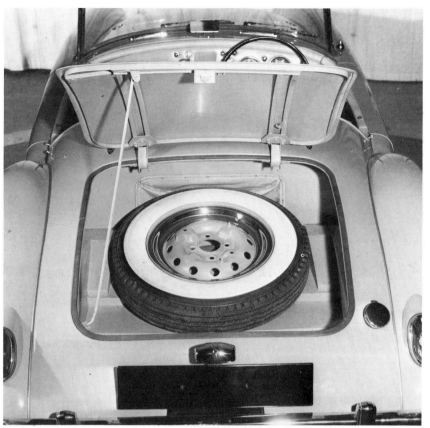

The MGA had limited luggage space, much of the compartment being taken up by the spare wheel. It was, perhaps, inevitable that a car which had originally been inspired by a special Le Mans entry should in due course return to the circuit as a production racer. The upper picture opposite shows some of the modifications made to the bodyshell, including the fairing over the passenger space to minimize drag, while the two lower pictures reveal a pair of the special Le Mans engines, which were developed with the collaboration of Harry Weslake, who by this time was acting as an air-flow consultant to BMC. Clearly visible on this page is the extension of the intake ports across the engine to the sparking plug side, where an external balance pipe has been fitted. The larger SU carburettors, with 1¾-inch diameter chokes, are another non-standard feature, while although the Le Mans cars, designated EX 182, had standard MGA transmission casings, they contained close-ratio gears.

193

The Longbridge-designed twin-overhead-camshaft engine, which was used only once in one of the EX 182 team cars prepared for the TT race at Dundrod in 1955. It was the rival Cowley-developed twin-ohc conversion, which also made its race debut in this event, which was to be adopted in due course for the production MGA Twin Cam.

Ken Wharton testing one of the EX 182 team cars at Silverstone before they were shipped over to Le Mans. Note the large-diameter auxiliary lamp recessed into one side of the radiator grille, the racing screen and the regulation bonnet fastenings.

A revealing overhead view of the production MGA chassis. A design requirement was that adequate space should be provided for the mounting of doors of substantial size. The siting of twin six-volt batteries ahead of the rear axle was a neat utilization of space, although it scarcely encouraged regular checks of the fluid level.

The front suspension of the MGA, showing how the lever-arm dampers are operated through the upper suspension links. The drum brakes, which identify this car as an MGA 1500, were replaced by discs when the car became a 1600, in 1959.

The B-series engine of the MGA was increased progressively in size by adopting a larger cylinder bore. The first stage was the increase from 1,489 to 1,588 cc, followed in 1961 by a further enlargement to 1,622 cc for the introduction of a Mark 2 version of the 1600, as seen here.

The cockpit of a production MGA. Detail changes from the layout of the prototype car illustrated earlier include a different rear-view mirror and three-wire instead of four-wire steering wheel spokes.

A competition windscreen was one of a wide list of high-performance equipment which was developed for the MGA.

This low-angle view illustrates the useful ground clearance which was provided with the MGA, a feature which some of its rival sports cars lacked to their detriment.

The bootlid-mounted luggage rack became a popular item of extra equipment with MGA owners who were anxious to supplement the rather meagre luggage space within the car.

The interim 1600 model, identifiable from its predecessor by the extra script on the bootlid and by the larger rear-light clusters.

Justifiably, the optional wire wheels were considered by many MGA buyers to be a most worthwhile extra for they did much to enhance the sporting pretensions of the model.

The MGA Coupe, which was introduced late in 1956, more than a year after the open two-seater's debut, was a refreshing example of the integration of closed bodywork into a sports car design. It sold at first at £699, £104 more than the open car. Vertically mounted exterior door handles were a novel touch, while the wrap-around three-section rear screen offered excellent visibility behind.

The MGA Coupe in left-hand-drive form and with the optional centre-lock wire wheels. The Coupe was attractively furnished and incorporated completely disappearing wind-down door windows.

As an alternative to the integrated body of the MGA Coupe, MG offered a detachable hardtop, with sliding door windows, as a fitment for the open two-seater. Here is an example fitted to a 1600.

Production of early MGAs at Abingdon alongside the assembly line for Z-type Magnettes and with the Riley Pathfinder line just visible in the background.

Celebrating the production of the 100,000th MG car on May 16, 1956. By the time production of the MGA had ended in 1962, more than 101,000 of this series alone had been manufactured.

Experienced and successful rally driver Nancy Mitchell, accompanied by Pat Faichney, just climbing aboard again, heading for the ladies' award in the 1956 Alpine Rally in the MGA which they had previously shared on the Mille Miglia and which sported a detachable hardtop for this event.

One of the EX 182 cars prepared originally for Le Mans, this example has subsequently been fitted with disc brakes and a twin-cam engine prior to the 1955 Tourist Trophy race, together with revised front-end bodywork to improve penetration.

The B-series engine in twin-carburettor form, as fitted to the MGA 1600, complete with clutch and gearbox assembly incorporating the remote-control selection mechanism.

The dashboard of an MGA 1600 Mark II in left-hand-drive form, with vinyl covering and with a matt-finished panel between the base of the screen and the top roll of the dashboard. This example has kilometre markings on the speedometer.

A Dunlop rear disc brake as fitted to the MGA Twin Cam in conjunction with Dunlop centre-lock ventilated disc wheels.

A Lockheed front brake disc assembly, which became standard equipment on the MGA when the 1500 model was replaced by the 1600 in 1959.

The development team behind EX 179, now with the cockpit on the right side of the car to accommodate the exhaust system of the twin-overhead-camshaft 1½-litre engine. Miles and Lockett were to collect 16 international class records with it, including the 12-hour at a speed of 141.71 mph and the 10-mile at a resounding 170.15 mph. On the right, the car is seen at rest on the salt prior to the speed attempts, while the lower picture was taken from the air and shows the car running close to a marker during the course of one of the endurance runs.

EX 179 was also equipped with a modified A-series engine for an attack on 1-litre records, and here Eyston, Wisdom and Ash celebrate their successes, which included an international class record for six hours at 132.13 mph, using a blown engine, plus the flying-mile at 143.47 mph, which was an American class record, while the 12-hour record was taken at 118.25 mph with an unblown engine.

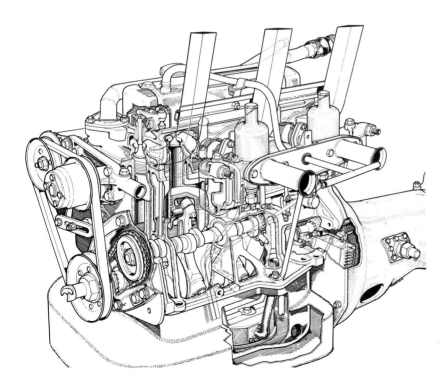

A cutaway drawing of one of the A-series engines used in EX 179. In this form, with a compression ratio of 10:1 and twin 1¼-inch SU carburettors, an output of 57 bhp at 5,500 rpm was obtained, while with the Shorrock-blown version, giving 4½ psi boost, the output was raised to 73 bhp at 5,500 rpm. A fuel consumption of 48.8 mpg was claimed during the course of the 12-hour endurance run.

The fruits of over 30 years of experience with small-engined but aerodynamically highly efficient record-breakers, EX 181 had a rear section designed to exert downward pressure without any additional spoiler. A small air brake was housed in the cockpit fairing and a carefully ducted engine radiator expelled just ahead of the exhaust.

The teardrop outline of EX 181 was the result of lengthy studies in the wind tunnel. More wheel movement was to be provided than on previous record cars.

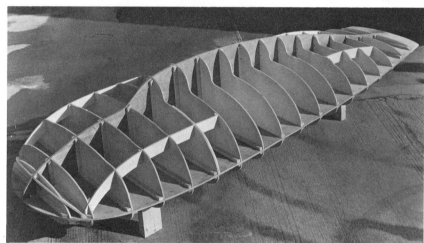

The MG twin-overhead-camshaft engine was fitted to EX 181 with a Shorrock blower designed originally for use with diesel trucks and feeding two 2½-inch SU carburettors at 32 psi boost. It produced an output of 290 bhp at 7,300 rpm.

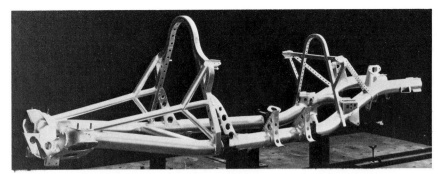

The robust and simple multi-tubular chassis-frame of EX 181.

At Utah in August 1957, after delays due to thunderstorms and in a failing light, Moss took EX 181 over a flying-kilometre at 245.6 mph to break the 1,500-cc record set by Gardner in 1939. A tailfin had been added for this attempt, and note also the horizontal steering wheel.

Two years later EX 181 returned to the salt flats with Eyston and Phil Hill to help publicize the introduction of the MGA Twin Cam. On this occasion Hill was timed at 254.9 mph over the distance — the fastest ever for an MG.

Just an idea. This attractive quarter-scale model, for wind-tunnel tests, was Enever's sports-racing project, coded EX 186, involving a 1956 adaptation of the EX 135/179 body with wrap-around screen and wheel cutouts. There would have been a twin-overhead-camshaft engine and de Dion rear suspension.

Nine years on, this full-scale wind-tunnel mock-up was produced, using standard MGB steel wheels, for a possible Le Mans project, which also never materialized.

This Frua version of the MGA, known as EX 214, had a rather cluttered front end, but some elements of this design were to find their way into production MGBs in due course.

The rear end of EX 214 was considerably cleaner, as well as offering a vastly increased luggage accommodation compared with the existing MGA.

The arrangement of the instruments of EX 214 within a pod immediately ahead of the driver was a feature adopted for the MGB, although inevitably the production car's interior was to be nothing like as ornate as this Frua suggestion.

Once the Pininfarina proposal for a four-door saloon had been adopted by the British Motor Corporation in the mid-1950s a process of badge engineering was put in hand whereby variations on the theme would be incorporated into the different marque catalogues. At one stage, as this artist's drawing makes clear, there was a suggestion that a Frua-style interpretation of the MG grille might be adopted . . .

. . . Fortunately, however, the idea was rejected and a more conventional design was adopted for integration into the Pininfarina shape. Here is a mock-up of the front end of the proposed MG saloon, which would mark another extension in the use of the Magnette name.

The production prototype of the Magnette Mark III, as it was to be known. Number plate dating experts should not be confused by the 'G' suffix. This was a made-up number, indicating ADO 9, the project number for all the 1½-litre saloons in this style, with G being the suffix letter for the MG version.

The well-balanced lines of the Pininfarina design at least had the merit that they stood the test of time, and the MG version was generally considered to be one of the better variations aesthetically. This picture, taken in 1961, is of a Mark IV, distinguishable from its immediate predecessor by the use of the upper body colour for the full length of the body instead of just the roof and rear wings.

The dashboard of the Mark III Magnette. The Mark IV version was almost identical except that the ignition lock was moved from the steering column shroud to the dashboard itself, alongside the toggle switches to the right of the driver on right-hand-drive cars like this.

The addition of wheel trims considerably enhanced the quality image of the Magnette Mark IV, production of which extended from 1961 to 1968.

Underbonnet accessibility was a strong point of the B-series-engined Magnettes. For the Mark III the engine was used in its original 1,489-cc form, giving 66.5 bhp at 5,200 rpm, but for the Mark IV the larger-bore 1,622-cc version was introduced, with the power output increased slightly to 68 bhp at 5,000 rpm.

Another important MG milestone, this time marking the production of the 50,000 sports car at Abingdon, although as can be seen from this picture, not all of them carried the MG badge. Austin-Healeys large and small were sharing the assembly lines in 1959. Below is one of the most coveted MGAs of them all, the Twin Cam, in open two-seater form. Only 2,111 Twin Cams were to be built between 1958 and 1960.

Jack Sears, Bob Olthoff and Sir John Whitmore with the team of three MGA 1600 Coupes prepared for the 12-hours endurance race at Sebring in 1962. Note the roof lights, additional driving lamps, the wider-spaced radiator grille bars and the additional ventilation grilles in the front body panels.

The previous year's Sebring entry was confined to a pair of Coupes on which, in contrast, the radiator air intakes had actually been reduced in size. Like the cars above, these Coupes looked at first glance to be Twin Cams, but were in fact 1600 De Luxe models equipped with the centre-lock wheels and disc brakes from the Twin Cam.

The exhaust side of the 1,588-cc engine of the Twin Cam with the four-branch manifold from the aluminium cylinder-head ready to accept twin downpipes.

The same engine from the induction side with the twin SU carburettors feeding straight and venturi-shaped inlet ports. Beefing-up of the bottom end to cope with the impressive power output of 108 bhp at 6,700 rpm included the use of 2-inch diameter main bearings and 1 7/8-inch diameter big-ends.

The bulkier dimensions of the Twin Cam engine made it quite a tight fit, and underbonnet accessibility as a result was considerably less favourable than with pushrod-engined MGAs.

Only minor changes in the dashboard of a Twin Cam identified it from other MGAs. The rev-counter read to 7,500 rpm, with the warning segments starting at 6,500 rpm, while the speedometer dial read to 120 mph.

The Mark II version of the MGA 1600 was announced in June 1961 with a B-series engine increased in capacity from 1,588 cc to 1,622 cc.

The main identification feature of the Mark II, which was also offered in Coupe form, was the modified radiator grille with recessed vertical bars, while identification lettering was also provided behind the ventilation grilles flanking the bonnet top.

Cousins, Enever and Thornley pose with another milestone MG, the 100,000th MGA to be produced at Abingdon, shortly before the model's production run came to an end in 1962. Appropriately, since the majority of the output had ended up there, the car was destined for the United States.

217

A variety of body shapes were considered in the search for a suitable replacement for the MGA including the wind-tunnel model above, which made use of a fully wrapped front screen, but which suffered from a rather over-ornate front end with bumpers integrated into the radiator grille surround. The lower example of a suggestion for a fastback hardtop was perhaps a little more acceptable, although this full-size mock-up gives the impression of being both too long and too heavy.

Another development exercise in 1959 was the creation of a possible MG open two-seater based on Mini components, which might become a substitute for the MG Midget derivative of the Austin-Healey Sprite. This styling buck reveals a pleasantly integrated appearance.

Side elevation of the MG proposal, which was based on the Minivan floor pan and was given the code number ADO 34.

Seen from the rear, the ADO 34 proposal incorporated a dashboard which seems to have been inspired more by that of the MGA than of the Mini saloon, while a useful amount of luggage accommodation was clearly in mind.

219

The MGB, the first MG sports car to feature unit construction of body and chassis, was a far more elegant design than some of the styling exercises which had preceded it might have led one to fear. White-wall tyres and left-hand drive leave one in no doubt as to where this car is heading.

The introduction of the MGB marked another increase in the capacity of the B-series engine, this time to 1,798 cc, resulting in a power improvement to 95 bhp at 5,400 rpm.

The wide engine bay of the MGB was a welcome feature of the new car, offering excellent working conditions for under-bonnet maintenance, although normally, of course, the top would not be supported open as widely as this.

Equally well received was the news that wire-spoke wheels would be offered as an option on the MGB, and a considerable proportion of the cars left the factory in this form.

The MGB was a spacious two-seater with ample room behind the two seats for additional luggage, especially if the optional hardtop was fitted, thereby obviating the need for hood stowage.

The cockpit of the MGB was a considerable change from that of the MGA and perhaps there had been just a little influence from that earlier Frua project, although the end result, happily, was far less ornate.

The detachable hood of the early MGBs and the folding arrangements for it meant that the luggage compartment was somewhat cluttered.

An American-specification MGB revealing the generous three-section rear windows let into the hood, offering excellent visibility, while the rear wing tips acted as convenient 'pointers' for reversing.

Developed from the original 'frog-eyed' Austin-Healey Sprite, but adopting the more conventional body shape provided for the Sprite Mark II, the MG Midget was powered initially by the A-series engine in its 948-cc form, offering a modest 46 bhp, but with the potential of much development. The standard of trim and equipment was subtly higher than for the equivalent Austin-Healey model.

Sprites and Midgets taking shape side-by-side in the Abingdon assembly area with an MGA line just visible in the background.

Early Midgets had detachable sidescreens with sliding glass panels and were devoid of exterior door handles. Apart from the different grille, chrome side body strips and one up the centre of the bonnet distinguished the Midget from the Sprite.

The front of an Abingdon-produced Sprite. This is one of the later 1,275-cc examples, with the revised windscreen to go with the wind-down door windows and with optional wire wheels.

A wire-wheeled Midget Mark III, with 1,275-cc engine delivering 65 bhp at 6,000 rpm, 6 bhp more than the 1,098-cc version which had powered the Mark II. By 1968, two years after its introduction, the Mark III had given way to the Mark IV, below, which was required to share a revised radiator grille with the Sprite, with just the central badge to distinguish them, much to the dismay of many MG enthusiasts.

Three delightful aluminium-bodied Midget coupes were built in 1962, two for Dick Jacobs' team to use in major British events, and this one for John Milne, of Scotland, seen here setting fastest time in his class, ahead of a Lotus Elan and two Jaguar E-types, on Rest and be Thankful in 1967.

Even in standard form, the Midget was a popular choice of motor sportsmen, especially for driving tests, and here David Robertson corrects a tail slide with his Mark III at Deanston, aided by the car's high-geared steering.

The Midget in early-1970s guise with rubber-faced overriders on the split bumpers which leave ample space for the rear numberplate between. The transverse run of the exhaust tailpipe and rear silencer is an interesting feature.

Rostyle wheels were standard equipment for the Midget in 1974 when this model, featuring round rear wheelarches, was produced. The Midget was to revert later to squared-off arches in order to provide extra crash resistance.

The interior of a 1974-model Midget, featuring a different steering wheel, a black crackle finish to the dashboard and head restraints for the seats.

After successive increases in power by adopting larger versions of the A-series engine — first of 948-cc, then 1,098-cc and ultimately 1,275-cc — a major change came for the Midget in 1975 when it was supplied with the 1,493-cc Triumph four-cylinder engine, as also used in the Spitfire sports car, although power output was scarcely changed from the previous engine.

From time to time special-equipment versions of the Midget were offered on the US market to stimulate sales, and this is an example from 1976, by which time the ugly but Federal-approved rubber bumpers had been adopted. The distinguishing equipment included wheel trim rings, an AM/FM radio, a chromed luggage rack and decorative flashes along the body sides.

Above, two views of the Longbridge styling version of ADO 34, the proposed MG derivation of the Mini, in which the relatively high nose necessary to clear the tall engine has been disguised very effectively. Like its Abingdon counterpart, however, the project was stillborn.

One of several attempts to make a GT coupe out of the MGA, this was a gallant effort by Douglas Wilson-Spratt, whose 1967 WSM used the MG's chassis structure with a light-alloy skin based on the lines of the Ferrari 250 GT.

Two MG models which did not emanate from Abingdon were the Longbridge-built 1100 and 1300 saloons. Here is a relatively rare export two-door 1100 raising the dust with Ken Fildes at the wheel in an autocross in Eire.

Walnut on the dashboard helped to give the Mark II MG 1300 saloon a quality image and enabled these saloons to become the biggest-selling MGs ever.

The traditional MG grille was made to blend in very neatly with the contours of this BMC body, which was also featured strongly in the Austin, Morris, Riley and Wolseley ranges. Front-wheel drive, Hydrolastic independent suspension and a transversely mounted engine — in this instance giving 58 bhp at 5,250 rpm — were features.

Completed MGB bodyshells coming off the line at the Pressed Steel Fisher factory in Swindon, from where they were sent to Cowley for painting and fitting of the hood before their final journey to Abingdon for finishing.

The end product after the Abingdon treatment, one of the most stylish open two-seaters of its time and a most worthy wearer of the MG badge.

A Cowley employee commissioned this special GT-style coupe body on the MGB before the classic Pininfarina-styled MGB GT, below, came on the scene. The Italian studio drew on a previous award-winning design built on an Austin-Healey chassis to achieve a harmonious unity between the basic MGB shape and the upper structure.

The businesslike layout of the MGBs used for the works rally teams was legendary, and this B-series engine with a Weber twin-choke carburettor is typical of equipment which was to become the ambition of so many rally enthusiasts.

The Morley brothers heading for the sun and success in the 1964 Monte Carlo Rally, when they took one of the best-known of the works MGBs, 7 DBL, to victory in the GT category.

The provision of an oversize fuel tank, complete with quick-action filler, on the works MGBs meant moving the spare wheel forward into the rear of the cockpit area.

Donald Morley working 7 DBL hard on the Monte Carlo street circuit to keep the MGB, fitted with a factory hardtop, ahead of one of the giant Ford Falcons from America.

Horses for courses, but in this case it is the same car. In the upper picture DRX 255C has been prepared for the 1965 Le Mans race with special long-nosed bodywork for Hopkirk and Hedges to drive it into a commendable 11th place overall at an average speed of 98.2 mph. For most of its hard-working life, however, this car, like the other works MGBs, reverted to its more conventional bodywork, as illustrated below.

Trevor and Anita Taylor took this factory hardtop-equipped MGB to second place in part one of the 1,000-miles endurance race at Brands Hatch in May 1965, beaten only by the similar car of Rhodes and Banks.

The so-called luggage compartment of one of the Le Mans-prepared MGBs, with the spare wheel, oversize fuel tank and quick-action filler taking up much of the available space.

Coming in for one of its many routine pitstops, this factory MGB was driven by Hedges and Vernaeve to outright victory in the 84-hours Marathon de la Route at the Nurburgring in 1966, and was the only survivor amongst the GT entries.

An interesting comparison between the standard MGB GT and the factory team car prepared for the 1967 season, as seen from the rear. The main differences are the external fuel filler and identification lights, the more convenient spare wheel mounting and, of course, the absence of the rear bumper from the competition car, which Hopkirk and Hedges drove into 11th place at Sebring. The same year, MBL 546E appeared as the first of the lightweight GTs which, amongst other changes, featured torsion-bar front suspension, as had been earmarked for the yet-to-be-announced MGC, and aggressively functional extended wheelarches to cover the Minilite wheels.

The interior of MBL 546E, which Hopkirk and Makinen shared in the 1967 Targa Florio, where the prototype car performed well to complete the course, although a troubled final lap cost it too much time to be officially classified.

Pending the arrival of the six-cylinder MGC engine, the lightweight prototype competed with a B-series engine bored out to give a capacity of 2,004-cc, thereby taking it into the over-2-litre class. In this form it produced approximately 150 bhp.

A happy retirement picture, taken in May 1966, of Syd Enever with the MGB GT with which he had been so closely associated and which was a most fitting tribute to his skill as MG's chief engineer.

The interior of the MGC, similar to that of the MGB apart from very minor differences such as the slightly longer gearlever. Another identification feature is the small bulge in the bonnet top, necessary to give adequate clearance over the induction side of the six-cylinder engine.

America's stringent regulations concerning crash protection encouraged MG to produce this radically altered cockpit for US-market MGBs and MGCs. The passenger gained a padded buffer, but lost a glove compartment, while part of the centre console had to be used for switches displaced from the centre of the dashboard.

One that got away. ADO 21 was a mid-engined car which might have been an MGB replacement, but by 1970 Triumph influence was strong and this exciting Abingdon-engineered project was shelved in favour of a more conentional sports car which ultimately appeared as the TR7.

The MGC in GT form took pride of place on the company's revolving turntable at Earls Court for its debut at the 1967 London Motor Show. Like the MGB, the car was offered with a choice of bolt-on disc or centre-lock wire wheels, but in each case their diameter was an inch greater at 15 inches.

The main external identification feature of the MGC had always been the raised centre-section of the bonnet top, supplemented by an additional small bulge on the left side.

The MGC in open two-seater form, riding slightly higher than an MGB and offering significantly better ground clearance than the Austin-Healey 3000, the car it was intended to replace.

As installed in the MGC, the C-series six-cylinder engine produced 150 bhp at 5,250 rpm and was normally coupled to a four-speed manual gearbox, for which overdrive was an option and three-speed automatic transmission an alternative specification.

A rare view of an MGC showing the layout of the torsion-bar front suspension, the anti-roll bar, the steering rack and the exhaust system.

Although the MGC only had a short, two-year, production life, a number of subtle changes were made to the detail specification in that time. The central locking nuts of the road wheels on this car, for example, have lost the ears which were present when the car was first announced — another concession to the growing mood of safety-consciousness.

Many changes were made to the interior of MGB models during their production life. This was the specification offered with the MGB GT in 1973, by which time the seats had been provided with brushed nylon on their wearing surfaces and the main switches were of the rocker type.

Apart from the very small difference in ride height, the only way to tell an MGC from an MGB GT was to read the lettering on the rear hatch.

Prepared for its race debut, the first of the lightweight cars, to become known unofficially at Abingdon as GTSs, still retained its conventional MG grille, but in due course this would be replaced by a simpler wire-mesh radiator protection.

Over-boring increased the capacity of the competition version of the C-series engine from 2,912 cc to 2,968 cc and with the aid of three Weber twin-choke 45-mm carburettors output was boosted to 202 bhp at 6,000 rpm.

Completed in time for the 1968 Marathon de la Route, from which it retired with engine trouble, this final GTS model was one of two prepared by the works for British Leyland's North American subsidiary to run in the 1969 12-hours race at Sebring, where Hopkirk and Hedges drove it into 15th place.

The MG GT lettering carried on the rear hatch of MBL 546E when it raced originally as an oversize MGB with the 2,004-cc B-series engine was retained even after the 3-litre engine was substituted following the announcement of the MGC. The car was shared by Vernaeve, Hedges and Fall for the 1968 Marathon de la Route on the Nurburgring . . .

...where, after climbing to third place and closing in on the leading Porsches, a brake problem cost the team a lot of time and after being driven round the daunting course with no braking power whatsoever the car finished a gallant sixth. Note the use of a quartet of auxiliary lamps and wire wheels for this endurance event.

The first major restyle of the front end of the MGB occurred in October 1969, when the traditional radiator grille gave way to this recessed design, while Rostyle wheels replaced the previous pressed-steel type, although wire wheels remained an option.

Similar changes were made to the GT version, this being a slightly later example which is carrying small rubber inserts on the front bumper overriders.

The late-1970 MGB being put through its paces and revealing that the front suspension offers a considerable degree of wheel travel with minimal body roll.

The recessed-grille period of MGB production lasted only until late-1972 when there was widespread relief amongst MG enthusiasts at the return to a more traditional design, although the vertical bars were gone forever, replaced by a discreet black mesh. The appearance of both the GT and the open two-seater was greatly enhanced by the change, but the Midget continued to be produced with a recessed grille, very similar to that of the Sprite.

Another MG celebration was justified in 1971 when George Turnbull, a boss of British Leyland at that time, went down to Abingdon to pose with the 250,000th MGB to be produced, 'Old No 1' being brought out of retirement for the day to do duty alongside the latest car.

The introduction of a Mark II version of the MGB, with all-synchromesh gearbox, coincided with the announcement of the MGC in 1967, for which automatic transmission was an optional extra, and the opportunity was taken to extend this option to the MGB as well. This is a 1970 example, with revised steering wheel, but with the radio loudspeaker still occupying the whole of the centre console.

A major British Leyland contribution to an international vehicle safety symposium held in 1972 was this MGB GT-based safety vehicle, known as SSV 1. Amongst its design features was a full passive restraint air-bag system, an automatically operated passive seat-belt system, anti-lock braking, heavily cushioned bumpers, anti-roll suspension, head restraints, a speed and station head-up display, an anti-crash bar behind the seats and Dunlop total-mobility tyres, soon to be developed as the Denovo series, with a run-flat facility.

A major development in 1973 was the installation of the Rover 3½-litre V-8 engine into the MGB GT shell to produce the sort of car aimed for, but never really achieved, with the MGC. In production for three years, the MGB GT V8 was almost entirely a home-market car, and only 2,591 examples were sold before it was withdrawn from production.

Apart from the additional badging on the radiator and the rear hatch, the MGB GT V8 was recognizable by the special wheels first seen on the SSV 1 research vehicle illustrated on the previous page.

As an interim measure to meet tightening regulations, MGBs were sent to the United States in 1974 with massive overriders on conventional bumpers, to the considerable disfigurement of the cars, but a more permanent solution was on the way.

The problem was overcome by a one-piece bumper-grille assembly which the stylists did their best to integrate into the overall profile of the MGB, with some success, but the passing of the conventional front-end treatment was widely mourned.

This side view of the 1975 MGB GT emphasizes the degree of front overhang which resulted from the introduction of the flexible front bumper/radiator moulding.

At least the new front end enabled the side and indicator lamps to be deeply recessed and therefore better protected from minor damage through parking errors.

The 1975 version of the MGB GT V8 after it, too, had been subjected to the flexible-bumper treatment, even though the car would never be sold on the United States market.

When the 50th anniversary of the MG sports car was celebrated in 1975, the opportunity was taken to produce a limited-edition Golden Anniversary version of the MGB GT in dark green and gold and with the wheels previously only available on the V-8-engined model. By this time, the standard MG range consisted of four models, and the Midget had followed the larger cars in having its own version of the flexible-bumper treatment.

One of the more startling developments in the life of the MGB came in the summer of 1976, so far as trim was concerned, with the introduction of brightly striped seat facings, a feature which was to meet a very mixed reception.

With the revised seating came another change in dashboard layout, with the instruments now recessed into the main facia moulding and visible through a new design of four-spoke steering wheel.

Inevitably, much of the competition activity with MGs during the 1970s was centred on the United States, and one of the most successful competitors, driving the Huffaker Engineering MGB, was Terry Visger, seen here at the 1977 SCCA run-offs at Road Atlanta, when he won the E-Production-class National Championship for the third time in succession.

The Royal Silver Jubilee year, 1977, provided the opportunity for MG to highlight the progress made in 25 years in the automotive field by photographing a TF Midget, the current car in the Coronation year, alongside the MGB GT.

Nearing the end of the road, in this case a minor road in Oxfordshire, one of the last MGBs, identifiable by its five-spoke road wheels, photographed as the gates of Abingdon were about to be closed in October 1980.

A final run of limited-edition open two-seaters and GTs marked the end of MGB production. Of the 420 bronze-finished sports cars, 212 had alloy wheels and 208 had the wire type. All 580 GTs had alloy wheels and all were finished in pewter metallic paint.

A sad sight in the winter of 1980-81 as the last of the MGBs are lined up in the compound adjacent to the now closed factory, awaiting delivery to their customers.

While Alan Curtis and his consortium were trying to put together their ultimately unsuccessful attempt to buy MG from BL Cars, Aston Martin Lagonda built a mock-up version of the MG tourer to demonstrate what could be done to update the car without involving ruinously expensive modifications. William Towns, designer of the Lagonda Bulldog, incorporated the GT windscreen and doors and cut back the deformable front bumper to introduce the rump of an old radiator grille surround. There was also a second skin on the lower body panels as well as special alloy wheels. The car had an interesting profile, both front and rear, but it was not to be.

In an effort to keep the MG name alive in Abingdon, first Mallalieu Cars and later Abingdon Classic Cars had plans to produce this special SEC version of the MGB in conjunction with the MG Owners Club, the first example being shown at the Classic Car Show at Earls Court late in 1980. There was talk of several versions, including the possibility of turbocharging, and several new and used cars were given the SEC treatment during 1981.

The original SEC MGB nearing completion at Abingdon, with the people responsible behind it. The more luxurious interior included walnut veneer facings on the dashboard, the hood was more carefully tailored than previously, the car reverted to the classic radiator grille and bumpers and the ride height was brought back to its pre-Federal settings, while the wire wheels were heavily chromed.

Another reminder of what might have been. This was EX 234, a car designed to accept a variety of engines, thereby obviating the need to have separate designs for replacements for the Midget and the larger sports cars. As originally conceived, there would have been independent Hydrolastic suspension on a slightly shorter floorpan than that of the MGB. The elegant styling was by Pininfarina and it reflects somewhat his work on the Alfa Romeo spider of the late-1960s. MG certainly had its full share of 'what-might-have-beens'.

The last of the Abingdon line . . .

The final MGB to be made to US specification was bought by Henry Ford II for inclusion in the Ford Museum at Dearborn, Michigan, where it was to join the original MG exhibit, an M-type owned by Edsel Ford and said to be the first of the marque to have gone to the USA. This black LE roadster is being handed over to Mr Ford by Graham Whitehead, chief executive of BL's North American subsidiary company, with the Detroit Renaissance Center forming an appropriate backdrop.

. . . but not the last of the MGs

On May 5, 1982, the MG name was reborn, not with a car from Abingdon, but with a special up-market, high-performance version of the Longbridge-built Metro. Distinguished by its special alloy wheels and tailgate spoiler, its 72-bhp version of BL Cars' A-Plus 1,275-cc engine offered a top speed of 101 mph, making it the fastest production MG saloon ever. More important, its combination of refinement and zest was true to the MG tradition, and as if to emphasize the fact, the MG octagon was well in evidence throughout the car. The qualities which had been synonymous with Abingdon for so many years were being preserved, and there was widespread pleasure amongst the most fervent MG enthusiasts, not simply that the marque name would live on, but that it would do so with a range of cars — the MG Metro 1300 was just the first of the new line — worthy of the famous name and badge. Let two of the staunchest MG devotees have the final word. After a preview of the new car Bill Wallace, chairman of the MG Car Club, said: 'How good it is to see the MG marque back in the European market and especially as it is on such an appropriate vehicle with safe handling allied to good performance. I hope we will go on to see many more MG models in the future.' And Roche Bentley, founder and secretary of the MG Owners Club, said: 'I found the MG Metro fun to drive, especially as it handled so well. It is a sporty model in every sense of the word and I am delighted that the MG marque lives on in such a worthy car.'